THRESHOLD
RESISTANCE

THRESHOLD RESISTANCE

The Extraordinary Career of a Luxury Retailing Pioneer

A. Alfred Taubman

Collins

An Imprint of HarperCollinsPublishers

FIRST EDITION

THRESHOLD RESISTANCE. Copyright © 2007 by A. Alfred Taubman.

HarperCollins books may be purchased for educational, business,
or sales promotional use. For information, please write:
Special Markets Department, HarperCollins Publishers,
10 East 53rd Street, New York, NY 10022.

Designed by Nicole Ferguson

Library of Congress Cataloging-in-Publication
Taubman, A. Alfred.
Threshold resistance : the extraordinary career of
a luxury retailing pioneer / A. Alfred Taubman.
p.   cm.
ISBN: 978-0-06-123537-5
ISBN-10: 0-06-123537-7
1. Taubman, A. Alfred.   2. Businessmen—United States—Biography.
3. Entrepreneurship—United States—Biography.
4. Architects—United States—Biography   I. Title.
HC102.5.T28A3 2007
381'.1092—dc22
[B]   2006049739

07 08 09 10 11 DIX/RRD 10 9 8 7 6 5 4 3

— CONTENTS —

Introduction *viii*

1. From Pontiac to Ann Arbor *1*

2. Creating My Own Path *9*

3. The Golden West *15*

4. Evolution of the Arcade *25*

5. Creating 100 Percent Locations *30*

6. Buying the Ranch *42*

7. A Frosted Mug of Root Beer *56*

8. Minding the Store *64*

9. Fashion Statement *73*

10. Sold! 84

11. Cookie Jars and Irises *95*

12. Selling Art and Root Beer *109*

13. Going Public *119*

14. The Best and Worst of Times *134*

15. Standing Alone *146*

16. *United States of America v. A. Alfred Taubman* *161*

17. 50444-054 *174*

18. Coming Home *187*

Epilogue *199*

Index *201*

Notes *212*

— ACKNOWLEDGMENTS —

Developing a regional shopping center requires the talents of many people. I can now say the same is true of writing a book.

I first want to thank Malcolm Gladwell, who I met in 2004, for giving me the inspiration to tackle this project and focus my story on the concept of threshold resistance. Christopher Tennyson, who has provided communications counsel to me and my companies for 23 years, helped me organize my thoughts and remember all the good and the bad. My longtime assistant, Melinda Marcuse, was a great fact-checker and sounding board. Helen Rowe patiently sorted through decades of photos, correspondence and news clippings. Each draft was constructively critiqued by my wife Judy and my attorney Jeffrey Miro (it takes a confident man to involve his wife and lawyer in the same project).

The enthusiastic Harper Collins team, headed by Marion Maneker, was indispensable, as was the skillful editing of Dan Gross. And my friend Mort Janklow skillfully guided us through the fascinating process of getting a memoir published.

Thanks also to Pauline Pitt and Tommy Kempner—the only two people nasty enough to publicly express their dislike for me during the most trying days of my life—for their unintended inspiration. Pauline was kind enough to describe me as a "pig" in the *New York Post* (actually, pigs are the most intelligent of all farm animals, with brains nearly the size of a human's) and Tommy sought me out personally at a dinner party to tell me how delighted he was that I was headed to prison.

In keeping with the spirit of the book, any profits I receive from its sale will be contributed to the University of Michigan ALS Clinic, where neurologist Dr. Eva Feldman and her medical research team are closing in on groundbreaking treatments.

Finally, I must single out my dear friend and partner Max Fisher, who passed away in 2005 at the impressive age of 96. Not a day goes by that I don't miss hearing from Max.

– INTRODUCTION –

"This better work, kid. It's your ass if it doesn't."

Strong words. Especially when you consider that they were directed at a twenty-four-year-old store planner by Milton J. Petrie, founder and chairman of the Petrie Stores Corporation. It was 1948, and I had just presented Petrie with an alternative plan for an apparel store he intended to build in Highland Park, Michigan, a close-in suburb of Detroit.

Petrie was a big wheel in retailing. Starting with a single hosiery shop in Cleveland in 1932, he had essentially invented the women's specialty store business in America and knew a good deal about how to design and build stores. By the time we met, he had hundreds around the country. What was wrong with the basic design his company had relied on so successfully? And what did a junior draftsman half his age at the Charles N. Agree architecture firm know that he didn't?

Here's what. The classic 5,000 to 6,000-square-foot Petrie store employed what we called a "deep throat" entry space bracketed by display windows. The front door was set in ten to fifteen feet from the sidewalk, which allowed the customer to view the merchandise leisurely in the windows before actually pushing the door open. Often, there was a glass-covered display island in this space as well. In theory, a shopper, protected in this initial U-shaped display space from the weather and the activity of the street, would enter the shop having already begun to make her purchase decisions.

That was the theory, anyway. But I didn't buy it. I may not have owned any stores at the time, but I had been selling things—shoes, clothes, flowers—to people since I was a kid. I had studied design in college and had some experience in the field. And where Petrie saw a tried-and-tested recipe for retailing success, I saw an inefficient use of space; where Petrie's experienced store designers saw opportunity, I saw unnecessary barriers. First, the deep window displays robbed precious interior sales space. Second, the idea of retailing is to get people *inside* the store. And the distance from the sidewalk to the front door only heightened the odds against the customer ever coming into the air-conditioned space where the salespeople had a chance to assist. Third, it was an aesthetic mess. The sheer amount of display space was difficult and expensive to maintain in an attractive and imaginative way. Dressing store windows is an art.

Petrie Stores was a critical tenant for our client's three-store retail development, and I certainly didn't want to mess things up. (Our client was Ira Gumm of Alpena, Michigan, who happened to be Judy Garland's uncle.) But I had to communicate my point of view.

I had presented an alternative design that featured more shallow, see-through display windows and a welcoming front door on the sidewalk, closer to the property line. This would create significantly more sales space and turn the store itself—with its merchandise, human activity, and light in full view—into the display. Most important of all, in my design, far less stood between the customer and the goods, the customer and the salespeople, the customer and a sale!

"In short, Mr. Petrie," I explained (we were not yet on a first-name basis), "we can eliminate much of the threshold resistance."

"Threshold resistance," he repeated slowly. "What do you mean by that?"

"The physical and psychological barriers that stand between your shoppers and your merchandise," I explained. "It's the force that keeps your customer from opening your door and coming in over the threshold. I think we can reduce all that with this new design."

What followed seemed like the longest period of silence in my life. Had I insulted this retailing icon? Had I jeopardized a leasing deal for one of my employer's most important clients? Come to think of it, who the hell did I think I was? All I could think about as Petrie stared at the blueprints laid out in front of him was how I was going to tell my fiancée that I had been fired.

But that's when those glorious words came out of his mouth: "This better work, kid. It's your ass if it doesn't."

You could say things worked out well. I kept my job at Agree, and Petrie Stores' Highland Park location became one of the strongest-performing stores in the chain, influencing future planning and design throughout the company. From that initial meeting, Milton Petrie and I developed a close friendship, which continued to the day he died, in 1994, at the age of ninety-two. In the intervening years, Milton was my neighbor in New York City and Palm Beach, one of the largest tenants in my shopping centers, and my partner in such business ventures as the Irvine Ranch and Sotheby's.

Our important encounter in 1948 also helped give me the confidence, after a short stint with the O. W. Burke construction company, to start my own real estate development business two years later. That enterprise, the Taubman Company, also worked out well. Over more than half a century, we have pioneered the development of shopping centers, transformed the nature and experience of luxury retailing, and created tens of thousands of jobs. Today, Taubman Centers owns and/or manages twenty-three large centers in the United States. If you've ever shopped at the Mall at Short Hills in New Jersey, or the Beverly Center in Los Angeles, or the Mall at Wellington Green in West Palm Beach, or the Cherry Creek Shopping Center in Denver, you've spent some time with us.

Developing unique retail environments certainly made me

wealthy—wealthier than I could have ever imagined. Equally important, it opened up a similarly unimaginable range of opportunities for me: to travel and see the world; to pursue my passion of collecting fine art; to meet and work with many of our time's leading entrepreneurs, businesspeople, artists, and civic leaders; to own a champion professional sports team; to get involved in businesses ranging from A&W Restaurants to Sotheby's; to contribute to the well-being of institutions and communities that made my career possible; and to create entities—buildings, companies, educational organizations—that will last far beyond my lifetime.

Now, the world surely doesn't need another book written by an older man telling how he became a self-made billionaire. In this country, and in this system under which we are blessed to live, it's relatively easy to make money.

So what's the point of this volume? Partly, it's that when you get to be my age, there's only so much golfing, fishing, and shooting you can do. Partly, it's to set the record straight and tell my side of the story after many years during which others—and frequently others who didn't know me or who intended to harm me—loudly trumpeted their versions of my life and career.

But mostly it's because I want to share what I've learned from my experiences. It's a safe bet most readers will never build a shopping mall or buy an auction house—or spend part of their retirement in a federal prison. Nonetheless, I've concluded that my experiences—my ups and downs, my gains and losses, my victories and defeats—allow me to offer some valuable perspective.

And looking back, it's clear to me that threshold resistance has been the key. In all my endeavors, in every chapter of my life, every relationship I've formed, every business opportunity I've pursued, every challenge I've encountered, every achievement I've enjoyed, threshold resistance has played a formative role.

It's always there, in business and in life. And it's not just about store design. Every day, we encounter psychological, physical, cultural, social, and economic barriers. In order to accomplish anything, people have to find a way to get beyond the limitations they believe that personal background, conventional wisdom, common practice, or experience has placed on their imaginations. Threshold resistance might stop a customer from entering a hosiery store. But it might also stop a young woman from applying to medical school, or stop an engineer with a great idea from leaving the comforts of a job to start his own company, or stop a politician from seeking votes among a vital growing constituency. For everybody, being able to assess and overcome threshold resistance is nothing less than an essential life skill.

If there's one thing I've learned over the years, it's that to succeed, you have to look beyond immediate barriers and see opportunities. Successful entrepreneurs and builders possess a sort of serial vision that allows them to look past things as they are to see how they could be better, not just different—and hence more valuable. It means looking at a wheat field in a rural area and seeing a massive shopping center that will serve a large local residential population. It means looking at a huge ranch in Southern California and seeing one of the nation's most prosperous and valuable real estate markets. It means looking at a snooty, off-putting fine-art auction house and seeing an open, inclusive retail business. And it means looking at seemingly intractable problems—the persistence of low achievement in public education, the economic struggles of Detroit—and seeing the possibility for change.

Spend a few hours with me, and I'll tell you how I encountered and overcame threshold resistance. I can't promise that my story will help you make more money or be more successful in your career. This isn't that kind of book. But I can guarantee you will learn a great deal. I know I have.

~ ONE ~

From Pontiac to Ann Arbor

I was born in 1924, five years before the start of the Great Depression, in Pontiac, Michigan, to German Jewish immigrants Fannie and Philip Taubman. Talk about threshold resistance. My parents surely encountered their fair share.

The story of how my parents came to America is a little hazy, as many immigrant stories are. From what I recall, my paternal grandfather was in the hardwood business in Bialystok, a city in what is today northeastern Poland that was known at the time for its textile industry and hard-working Russian, Polish, Jewish, and German population. In the first decade of the twentieth century, the story goes, he sent my father to the United States to find supplies of wood. My father came via boat up the Mississippi River and landed in Davenport, Iowa, where he was to meet an agent who would take him to Wisconsin and Minnesota. But my father, who spoke not a word of English, arrived on a Sunday, and the agent didn't show up, so he was promptly put in jail. The agent eventually showed up, got him out of jail, and helped him get a job as a gear grinder in a factory. After about a year, his parents were concerned that he might marry a non-Jewish woman, and so they sent over his second cousin—my mother—to keep him from straying.

They married, settled down in Davenport, and started a family. My oldest sister, Goldye, was born in 1913 followed by two boys, Sam and Lester, in 1915 and 1920. My father worked for the Wilson Foundry Company, and after World War I he was transferred to Wilson's Pontiac plant on Saginaw Street. My father had a good job with Wilson. The company thought highly enough of him to transfer him to its growing Michigan operation. But my father never felt satisfied or safe. He never fit in with the top executives, who certainly were not Jewish immigrants and were not about to invite him to join their country clubs. My father had dreams, ambition, and a desire to provide the best for his family. Call it entrepreneurial intuition: he knew there were at least as many barriers to his success at Wilson as there were opportunities.

Blessed with true entrepreneurial guts and spirit, my dad left the relative safety of the corporate world to start small fruit farms in nearby towns like Rochester and Orion. Later, he built modest commercial real estate projects and custom homes, including the comfortable four-bedroom Tudor-style home at 300 Ottawa Drive in which I was born. He also built the first synagogue in Pontiac. Both the house and the synagogue still stand.

The region was booming in the 1920s, as companies like Pontiac Motor, Oakland Motor, and Ford built plants that created thousands of well-paying jobs. A guy from New York named Shutzie had talked my father into building houses on some land just north of Pontiac, so he and my father borrowed money from the bank and put up a bunch of homes. Then the crash came, bringing widespread unemployment. In those days, the name of the original home builder remained on a mortgage even after the house was sold. If the home owner stopped making the mortgage payments, the bank looked to the builder for the funds. (Later, legislation was passed to include exculpatory clauses in mortgages to limit the builder's responsibility to the bank once the house was sold.) So when people who were unable to pay their mortgages walked away from their homes, the bank looked to my father for repayment. Shutzie left town and went to Los Angeles.

My father was stuck with these vacant houses, which he couldn't sell or rent out. But he refused to abandon his financial obligations. For a period, he tended his orchards in northern Oakland County and moved us into a modest cottage on Sylvan Lake. Though it took him many years, my father made good on every precrash debt he owed, even though dozens of clients had left him holding the bag. It was a big lesson to us all. I remember those years as a very difficult period. I recall visiting a friend of mine—his father was an architect—and seeing him burning furniture in the fireplace for heat because their gas had been cut off.

School was not easy for me, either. To the best of their ability, my siblings helped pave the way for me. Back then, dyslexia, which I have struggled with all my life, was diagnosed as slowness or stupidity. As a kid I also stuttered. Add the fact that I was always big and a bit awkward for my age, and you get the idea that I was not a model student.

There were two things we always had in abundant supply at home during those challenging years: our love and our faith. In Pontiac we were part of a small but tightly knit Jewish community of about sixty families. My parents would send my sister to the West Side of Detroit once a week to get kosher meat. Most years at school, I was the only Jewish kid in my class. My parents spoke German at home. And with my name—I was called Adolph Alfred after my two grandfathers, who were both named Avram—I definitely had the sense of being an outsider. I was a big kid, though, which helped keep me out of a lot of fights. And thanks to some gifted, dedicated teachers in the Pontiac public schools, I never lost my sense of curiosity and desire to learn. Where others saw challenges, my teachers saw potential. I think that's why I so respect the teaching profession and have made education a major focus of my philanthropy.

Even at a very young age I was aware of the barriers—threshold resistance—I would have to overcome to enjoy the level of success I could only dream about. Early on, I discovered that hard work broke through a lot of those hurdles. If it took me all night to read a simple chapter in a textbook, I put in the time. For spending money I caddied at local golf courses when I was nine years old. You could make $1.10 for eighteen holes.

I also learned some early lessons about what works in retail. From age eleven through high school I worked afternoons and weekends in Sims, a discount department store on Saginaw Street in Pontiac. They were smart merchants, selling inexpensive goods for working people. I learned a valuable lesson one day when an irate mother came into the store to complain about a pair of shoes I had sold her for her young son a few weeks earlier. The boy had very narrow feet, and I had fit him terribly. I gave her a new pair and offered to have the cost taken out of my pay. The Simon brothers, who owned the store, immediately took me up on my offer.

At Sims I learned how to seductively display a tie with a new shirt, suggest a second pair of shoes, and recommend a color to complement a particular skin type. Selling was fun, and I was good at it. I also learned to recognize the difference in quality between one garment and another. Single-stitch sewing made all the difference in a dress shirt's look and life. Cheaper double-stitched shirts, which creased and bunched at the seams, became rags after a few washings. Unless a customer needed his new shirt only for church on Sundays, the savings for a cheaper shirt never made sense. It was satisfying to help shoppers through these important decisions and earn their trust. It was a great feeling to have customers come into the store and specifically ask for me— especially if they asked one of the Simon brothers!

After graduating high school in 1942, I enrolled at the University of Michigan to study art and architecture. But before I could learn the words to the fight song, geopolitics altered my agenda. After Japan bombed Pearl Harbor, on December 7, 1941, my buddies and I couldn't wait to enlist. We naively feared that the war would pass us by if we didn't hurry. There certainly was no lack of clarity regarding our country's reasons for taking on the Japanese and the Germans. It was around this time that I stopped using my first name, Adolph.

I entered the Army Air Corps in 1942, hoping to become a pilot. But a near-fatal accident during flight training in Oklahoma convinced me I was better off and more useful to Uncle Sam in intelligence, principally charting, mapping, and taking aerial photographs to assess after-action damage. My service with the Thirteenth Air Force was in the Pacific theater—New Caledonia, New Guinea, Guadalcanal, and Okinawa. We'd fly out several times each week and come back exhausted. And in the middle of the night, Japanese planes would come and drop a few antipersonnel bombs, just to keep us up. My most vivid memory is of the devastation I saw and reported over Hiroshima, Japan, in the weeks after the first atom bomb was dropped in August 1945 (a second bomb would be deployed over Nagasaki three days later). Typically, I could confirm hits and damage to key targets by identifying landmarks and lining up street grids. That day in the heart of the city there were no surviving landmarks and no street grid. Seen from ground level, the destruction in Japan was even worse. I remember driving from Tokyo to Yokohama in a jeep. There were no highways, so we followed the surface streets. The street patterns were immaculate. All the houses had burned down, and only the chimneys remained standing. We drove for miles and miles and didn't see any people. I pray that our planet will never see anything like that again.

When I came home from the war at the end of 1945, I returned to the University of Michigan in Ann Arbor with some assistance from the GI Bill. It wasn't the typical college experience. To begin with, I was twenty-one and in a hurry to get on with my life. I joined a fraternity, Phi Sigma Delta, and became head of the food department, which meant I got free meals. I enrolled in the architecture school and enjoyed the classes. At the time, the architects teaching us had been trained in the Beaux-Arts school, so we were taught to draw the great cathedrals like Chartres and Notre-Dame, with their flying buttresses and trusses. I also dabbled a little in painting.

Carlos Lopez was one of my favorite professors at the University of Michigan. He taught a painting course in the fine arts department and was an accomplished artist himself. Unfortunately, much of the time I should have been in class learning from Professor Lopez, I was on the golf course or looking after one of my fledgling campus businesses. Nevertheless, I loved his course and enjoyed painting very much.

At the end of the semester, as grades were being finalized, Professor Lopez called me to his office to give me two things I'll never forget: a C and a drawing. The C, he explained, was the highest grade he could muster, given my regular absence from class. The drawing, one of his own india ink and wash depictions of a falconer, was a gift to encourage my continued interest in art.

"You have promise, Alfred," I remember him saying, "but you will not find it on the golf course."

The wonderful drawing, the first piece of art I ever owned, still hangs in my home. And the professor's words still ring in my ears. Since that humbling meeting more than a half-century ago, my golf game has shown more deterioration than brilliance, but my love of art has blossomed into one of the joys of my life.

I did spend some time on the golf course, but I also spent a lot of time working. I always had a few jobs during school. With no money for anything other than tuition, I immediately visited the local shoe store and offered the proprietor a proposition that was either creative or desperate. Instinctively understanding that convenience trumps threshold resistance, I would visit the on-campus sorority houses just after dinner with an assortment of stylish women's shoes from the store's inventory. With the permission of the housemothers, I displayed the shoes on the stairway leading up to the girls' rooms. As they finished dinner, they would pass by my display, I would take orders, and they would pay for and pick up their new shoes at the store in town over the next few days. I would hand the girls a slip of paper designating the style and size of their shoes. I always guessed their size correctly (honestly, I never missed), but the girls didn't see the size on my order slip. I had devised a graph (styles down one column, sizes across the top) with the store owner to create a code only we could decipher. Believe me, nothing kills a sale faster than suggesting to a girl who wants to be a size six that she really is a size nine.

Shoes at that time ran about $18 to $26. I could sell a dozen pairs each night, netting $1 per pair. If the shoe was a slow-selling model, the store owner gave me a bonus of 50¢. Not a bad way to make ends meet and meet girls at the same time!

My experience as a shoe salesman came up decades later in 2003 at a conference in Philadelphia sponsored by the University of Pennsylvania Wharton School's Samuel Zell and Robert Lurie Real Estate Center. Professor Peter Linemann invited me to participate on a "Living Legends" panel with real estate giants Gerald Hines and Walter Shorenstein. And it turned out that the three of us had worked as shoe salesmen early in our careers. Linemann asked if there was some lesson to be learned from our shared experience. Gerry and Walter did their best to stay serious, but I couldn't help myself. "Looking back," I answered, "I can say that the best thing about being a shoe salesman was the view." After a few awkward seconds of pondering my reply, the audience roared with laughter. Thank goodness.

I also got into the wholesale business. Around prom season at the University of Michigan I assembled a sales force of fellow undergraduates to stream through the dormitories and fraternity houses, taking orders for corsages, which I priced well below the local florist. On prom day, I would drive to Detroit's Eastern Market to buy the corsages wholesale, rush back to campus (at least, as fast as my finicky 1940 Ford would take me), where my sales team was waiting, equipped with a fleet of bicycles. Orders were delivered fresh right to the customers' doors.

I didn't know it at the time, but I was developing my own theory of threshold resistance throughout these formative years. I saw opportunities where others hadn't. I learned the value of service and convenience, as well as presentation and delivery to pull the customer toward a new opportunity. I learned that a lack of capital was no barrier to entry if you had a good idea. And I learned that my strengths were far more important than my shortcomings, and that even the most difficult personal and business challenges—whether physical or psychological—could be overcome if understood and confronted forcefully.

I learned something else about myself in those years, too: I was impatient. I was eager to get out and take advantage of what I saw as a world of opportunity. And so I left Ann Arbor (with three years of credits, thanks to my war service) and enrolled in night school closer to Detroit at Lawrence Tech to continue my architectural training. I proposed to my college sweetheart, Reva Kolodney, and went to work for Charles N. Agree.

So by the time I mustered the confidence to hand Milton Petrie the sketches for my alternative store plan, things were beginning to fall into place.

− TWO −

Creating My Own Path

Why do people start their own businesses? Do entrepreneurs share certain personality traits? What motivates someone to abandon the predictable safety net of corporate life? Academic scholars are just now beginning to study these issues in a systematic way. I've never taken a scientific survey, but from a lifetime of close observation, I've reached a few of my own conclusions. I think men and women who go it alone in business are different. Because of that, they're also very insecure, which is not always a bad thing.

At root, it's really not about a propensity or a desire to take risks. No, it's about a different perception of what risk means. Entrepreneurs often see staying put as a more risky proposition than moving on. That's certainly how my father saw things, and I know it's how I approached life. For whatever reasons, many entrepreneurs don't grow up comfortably fitting in. I certainly didn't. Some are shy, others physically unattractive, many are from dysfunctional or disadvantaged family backgrounds, and still others are just smarter than those around them. But unlike people who allow these types of challenges or differences to get in their way, entrepreneurs—regardless of race, religion, or gender—seem to understand that being different makes it necessary to create their own paths. That's a powerful motivation.

Creativity and optimism are other common traits among people who start businesses, found organizations, and push innovation. Ideas drive them. They want to be a certain type of person and achieve a special dream that keeps forming and calling to them in their minds. But growing up different has convinced them that the only person they can really count on to make it all happen is the person they look at in the mirror every morning.

In 1950, at age twenty-six, I turned to the guy in the mirror, and with a $5,000 loan from Manufacturers National Bank of Detroit (now part of Comerica), started paving my own path. I wanted to use everything I had learned at Sims, in school, in my military travels, and in my brief career in the field to design and build extraordinary retail properties. I wanted to create places where customers would want to shop and retailers would want to do business—more business than they had ever done before.

At this point, I felt that I had a decent amount of experience. I had worked as a draftsman and store planner for the architect Charles Agree. Agree specialized in retail, and I learned a great deal designing interiors for drugstores and department stores. We would work with tenants to determine where they wanted to locate key departments, and I began to understand the way retail traffic flows through a store. But I realized that while I enjoyed architecture and drawing, I really wanted to build. Part of it was for lifestyle reasons. I couldn't see anyone in architecture who had done well financially. I remember the great architect Frank Lloyd Wright coming to the University of Michigan and telling us that you could either marry somebody rich, inherit wealth, or starve to death. None of these seemed to me to be a viable option. And when I looked over the horizon, I saw that there was money to be made by people who could build and own stores or, better yet, groups of stores. And part of it was temperament. I preferred the energy and excitement of construction sites and negotiating deals to sitting at tables and drawing.

My first move was to leave Agree and join the construction firm O. W. Burke, where I began to supervise job sites and learn a great deal about how buildings are actually constructed. By 1950, I felt ready to go off on my own.

I ran the office, which we opened in Pontiac. My father, who was delighted to come out of retirement to be my partner, handled the field operations and provided some much-needed credibility with the bank. I looked young for my age in those days, and my dad brought some gray hair (and years of valuable experience) to the enterprise.

The partnership reminds me of an old joke.

A joint British-French panel is reviewing proposals to select the construction contractor for the massive "Chunnel" project. The largest construction companies in the world—several combining into consortiums—are bidding to construct this massive public works project. The tiny Cohen and Son Construction Company, of Queens, New York, is also bidding.

A skeptical judge asks the senior Mr. Cohen: "In your company's proposal you pledge to complete this work in half the time at less than half the cost of any other competitor. How could this be possible?"

"Very simple," responds Mr. Cohen with confidence and a thick Yiddish accent. "My son vill be stationed on the French side of the Channel, and I vill verk from the British side. Ven I say dig, ve dig! That way ve'll be done in half the time at half the cost."

"Mr. Cohen," the official asks, "what happens if you and your son fail to meet in the middle?"

"Then you'll have two tunnels for the price of one!"

Well, my father and I did not set out to join two continents, or to change the world. But we certainly put together our share of ambitious proposals. Our first job, however, was a modest free-standing bridal shop, Mrs. Ray's Bridal Salon, across from Federal's department store on Oakman Boulevard in northwest Detroit. The contract with Mrs. Ray (which I used as collateral for the Manufacturer's loan) called for design, construction, and fixturing—what we in the building trade call a turnkey job. Mrs. Ray, an authentic entrepreneur herself, could literally show up with her inventory and a cash register and be in business. The store was a big success and we had our first satisfied customer.

Fortunately, work came to us on a pretty steady basis during our first few years. We quickly graduated to department stores, an occasional hotel, and a few strip shopping centers. As our workload grew, so did our company. Dick Kughn joined us in 1955 as our estimator and would quickly become a partner and rise to the position of president, a position he held until he retired from the company in 1983. I was glad to have Dick on board. Being responsible for an ever-expanding family of employees was one of the most difficult aspects of business for me.

At our first company picnic, I remember looking out at the employees and their families on the lawn and seeing instead a very large nest of birds, all craning their necks, mouths wide open, calling for food. That's when it really hit me just how responsible I was for their well-being. If I screwed up, their children's teeth wouldn't be straight or white, and their mortgages wouldn't be paid. I knew I needed great people to help my business grow, and I deeply appreciated my employees' commitment, but the responsibility I felt for them and their families was at times overwhelming.

I still remember the feeling in the pit of my stomach when I received a phone call at home in the middle of the night from the father of one of our young secretaries. Our employees had all gathered earlier that evening at a restaurant in Detroit for our company Christmas party. Apparently, this young woman, who still lived with her parents, had decided to spend the rest of the evening with one of our not-so-young executives. That was the last company party we had for many years, and I made sure that everybody had Dick Kughn's home phone number.

I was pleased with my progress, professionally and personally. Reva and I were married in 1948 and settled in an apartment in Detroit. Our first child, Gayle, was born in 1951, and Robert followed in 1953. William completed our clan in 1958. But I was eager to take on larger building projects, and in 1953, I saw an opportunity. A friend from school, Irving Rose, pointed me in the direction of a troubled project in Flint, Michigan. An out-of-town developer was putting up a large (for the time) group of stores, anchored by a Federal's department store, but had made a mess of the design and execution. The original developer had designed it to connect to a nonexistent sewer in the street, to cite one example.

At the time, Flint was a growing and prosperous market, with its huge Buick plants. The Taubman Company stepped in and completed the project. And we did something comparatively radical: we moved the stores from the front of the lot to the back, and put the parking in front of the retail stores.

North Flint Plaza was a success and gave us the confidence to plot our own larger-scale developments. In 1957, we completed the forty-store Taylortown Shopping Center in Taylor, Michigan, and in 1959, we started work on our first large mall—the single-level Arborland, a large center near the University of Michigan campus, which included a Montgomery Ward, Kroger, JCPenney, and S. S. Kresge. We broke ground in early 1961 on the 350,000-square-foot project. Montgomery Ward alone took 120,000 square feet, and the entire project cost about $5 million. These were the first of what would prove to be a very fruitful and profitable line of business for the company.

In the mid-1950s, I also formed a friendship and partnership that would be as fruitful and profitable, economically and personally. Through doing business and living in the Detroit area, I had gotten to know Max Fisher, who was one of the most successful entrepreneurs in the state and in the country. Max, who had made a fortune in the oil industry, had acquired the Speedway chain of gas stations to distribute fuel from the successful refinery business he had built in Detroit during and after World War II. He asked me to help transform them from discounters into a new merchandising and service concept. I designed an innovative fascia treatment for the stations, using just-introduced outdoor fluorescent lighting (prior to this technological breakthrough, expensive, hard-to-maintain neon tubing was the only exterior option). By creating what was essentially a large plastic light box along the front of the service building, we dressed up the station with a brilliant illuminated sign for Speedway 79, easily read by motorists zooming by. Max eventually hired us to redesign and remodel a very large number of his stations. He became a lifelong friend, mentor, adviser, and partner.

By the end of the 1950s, we had certainly come a long way. The Taubman Company had evolved from a two-person upstart builder backed by $5,000 in debt to a developer with a substantial track record in Michigan and a healthy book of business. But our dreams were much bigger. And as it had to so many previous generations of adventurers, California beckoned us to go west.

THREE

The Golden West

Postwar America was booming. New housing developments were springing up everywhere. Highway systems were being constructed across the nation, and Detroit's factories were churning out automobiles around the clock for growing families. After nearly two decades of depression and war, an unprecedented national prosperity was creating the largest and most prosperous middle class any society had ever known, and a new phenomenon—television—was fueling a national desire for more and better consumer goods.

By this time, we could see that developing large-scale retail properties was a numbers game, a question of population (and population growth), income, distances, and roads. We had experienced and profited from this growth in Michigan, but we could see that other parts of the country were growing more rapidly, like California. I began to think about building there. But I faced a huge amount of threshold resistance. The logical place to expand for a company like ours would have been an adjacent area, such as northern Indiana or Chicago. We didn't have much in the way of experience, contacts, or reputation in California, but it seemed like a natural move for me. We were facing some resistance to further expansion in the Detroit area. Hudson's, the dominant department store chain in the region, didn't have any interest in working with me, and California was growing by leaps and bounds.

In 1959, I went to San Francisco to find a leasing company and met with old Mr. Coldwell at Coldwell Banker, who practically kicked me out of his office, saying, "I hope you bought a round-trip ticket out, because we don't need any shopping centers." I walked down Sutter Street and hired the Milton Meyer Company—a brokerage firm with a young leasing agent named Sheldon Gordon (who would become my lifelong friend and partner), and began to look for a large plot of land.

I found it in San Francisco's East Bay area, where we set out to do something revolutionary: build malls about twice the size as comparable ones and enclose them.

I can remember as if it were yesterday the first meeting I had in 1963 with James O. York, who was working on the Macy's account for a prominent market research firm. Jim had concluded from his analysis of population growth, highway patterns, and existing competition in the East Bay area that our proposed project—Sunvalley, to be built in the town of Concord—would be a great success. But he felt the center should be around 300,000 square feet total. He also recommended that the project's Macy's store be only 60,000 square feet.

I, on the other hand, was planning a center of 1.25 million square feet, including Sears, JCPenney, and a Macy's of more than 200,000 square feet. In other words, Jim and I were only about 900,000 square feet apart!

At the time, construction was already well under way at our first West Coast project, a much smaller mall thirty miles to the southwest, in Hayward, California. Southland, the first enclosed mall in northern California, opened in 1964, anchored by Sears, JCPenney and Emporium Capwell.

To understand the level of resistance to my plans, you have to consider the conventional industry wisdom at the time. Major department stores, in order to preserve the dominance of their flagship locations (in this case, the 600,000-square-foot Macy's store in down-town San Francisco), severely limited the size and merchandise se-lection offered in branch suburban locations. This strategy vastly underestimated the pace of population growth in suburban com-munities surrounding central cities and, ironically, threatened the very market dominance it was devised to protect.

Before I get back to my discussion with Jim, a bit of history will be helpful.

Many people to this day blame the suburban mall, at least in part, for the demise of America's downtowns. I have found throughout my adult life at cocktail and dinner parties that it is politically cor-rect to be prodowntown and antisuburb. Inner cities are alive with culture and sophistication; suburban communities are vacuous and homogenized. *West Side Story* vs. *Leave It to Beaver.* The "21" Club vs. Mc-Donald's. In fact, a popular myth holds that regional malls began to spring up in cornfields across America shortly after World War II, creating suburbia—an evil, all-powerful magnet that drew people, housing, and commercial development away from our nation's vul-nerable inner cities.

That's a distorted view of history. First of all, we need to recognize that settlers from the beginning of our nation's history established unique patterns of urban development far different from the Old World cities from which they fled. An urban study in the 1890s, a time when commuter railroads had already kickstarted the growth of sub-urbs, found that the population density of American cities averaged twenty-two people per acre, compared to 157 for cities in Germany.

America's affinity for a suburban lifestyle is certainly not a new aspiration. In fact, archaeologists discovered the following inscrip-tion on a clay tablet dating back to 539 BC:

Our property seems to me the most beautiful in the world. It is so close to Babylon that we enjoy all the advantages of the city, and yet when we come home we are away from all the noise and dust.

Nevertheless, we tend to focus on the 1940s and 1950s as the dawn of America's suburbs. Of course, by the 1920s, immigration, advances in mechanized farming, as well as the flow of returning servicemen from World War I, had created an unsustainable wave of urban population growth. Because our cities could not accommodate these numbers, growth migrated to the city's fringe. In response, retailers followed to conveniently serve customers in these new communities.

But as a general rule, the major department store companies—Dayton's in Minneapolis, Hudson's in Detroit, Wanamaker's in Philadelphia, Lazarus in Columbus, Marshall Field's in Chicago—stayed put in their protected downtown locations. For the first half of the twentieth century, established downtown department stores exercised significant control of land use and the political process. Politicians marched in store-sponsored holiday parades, and wings of hospitals were built with generous corporate contributions from retailers. These stores were among the largest employers and most visible local businesses. In 1953, Hudson's flagship store in downtown Detroit employed 12,000 people and maintained a delivery force of 500 drivers operating 300 trucks!

Because of this extraordinary influence and their ability to control the distribution of name brands, department stores were able to forestall competition from new retailers in their markets. America's cities were essentially one-store towns. Before landmark free-trade rulings in the 1960s and 1970s, if you wanted to purchase a Hathaway dress shirt in Detroit, you had to go to Hudson's—and only Hudson's. They, like powerful department stores in other cities, absolutely controlled distribution of the most popular apparel brands.

For decades, dominant department stores made it difficult if not impossible for upstart merchants such as Sears, Montgomery Ward, and other variety and specialty stores to secure competitive downtown locations.

Contrary to dinner party myth, retail *follows* residential growth.

People shop where they live, not necessarily where they work. As a result, upstart stores found locations called "hot spots" two, four, or six miles from downtown. These street-front properties were serviced primarily by foot traffic, buses, streetcars, and increasingly, automobiles. The irony? If department stores had not excluded competitors like Sears and JCPenney from downtown locations, fewer new retail developments would have been built to splinter the markets and challenge the flagships' dominance.

The automobile and the mobility it provided to America's growing middle class changed everything for the downtown department store. By 1930, 23 million cars were registered in America. And after World War II, federal programs offering affordable financing for new home-buyers and historic expenditures on highway construction accelerated the exodus of formerly captive customers. By the 1960s, major downtown department stores had no choice but to join the outcast family of chain stores in major new suburban centers like Southland and Sunvalley.

Of course, the department stores themselves played a significant part in the migration of retail to the suburbs. Some people credit Northland Mall, which opened in the Detroit suburb of Southfield in 1954, with being one of our nation's first regional shopping malls. What made the 1954 opening of Northland so pivotal to development patterns in southeast Michigan was the size of the Hudson's department store that anchored it. Now, it's understandable that Hudson's, the region's dominant retailer, would make the decision to build its second store beyond the city limits. All major department store operators were beginning to build branch stores in the suburbs by this time. What was unusual, however, was Hudson's decision to build such large stores—a 600,000-square-foot store at Northland and, in 1957, a 400,000-square-foot store at Eastland in Harper Woods. These were not branch stores, which typically were between 150,000 and 200,000 square feet. And they gave shoppers another reason to make purchases closer to where they lived instead of downtown.

I certainly wasn't alone in building large projects in different states. This period of explosive growth saw the formation of several shopping center companies that grew to be national firms, and there was plenty of room for all of us. On the West Coast, Ernest W. Hahn started his business in 1947 as a general contractor specializing in carpentry. Ernie handled the carpentry for me at Eastridge, which opened in San Jose in 1971. His first center, La Cumbre Plaza in Santa Barbara, opened in 1967. For a few years in the late 1990s, Taubman Centers owned the property along with the Paseo Nuevo center in downtown Santa Barbara. Hahn was one of the first mall developers to form a public company—the Hahn Company—which was ultimately acquired by Canadian real estate giant Trizec in 1980.

For whatever reason, the Midwest bred several mall pioneers. Matthew and Martin Bucksbaum, brothers originally from Iowa, formed what is today the very successful General Growth Properties in 1954 after trying his hand at managing a supermarket business. I made an offer to buy the Bucksbaums' portfolio in the late 1960s. They turned me down. And while the discussions were entirely friendly, I think I hurt their feelings. I didn't mean to, and to this day I deeply respect the family and their business.

Melvin Simon, along with his brothers, Herbert and Fred, started in the construction business in 1960 in Indianapolis. The Simons were from New York, but Mel's job as a leasing agent for Albert J. Frankel Co., a strip center developer based in Indianapolis, brought the family west. Edward J. DeBartolo of Youngstown, Ohio, formed his construction company in 1948 and soon branched out into retail development close to home and later in Florida. The DeBartolo Company was acquired by Simon in 1996.

Philip M. Klutznick, also a product of the Midwest, was born in Kansas City, in 1907. His father, Morris, was a cobbler. Philip and his family lived above the store—literally. A lawyer by training, Philip became a champion of public housing and was named commissioner of the Federal Public Housing Authority by Franklin Roosevelt in 1944. The opportunity to plan the model city of Park Forest, a suburb of Chicago, brought Philip to the Windy City after the war, where several Klutznick retail projects were developed in the 1950s. These centers were not enclosed. On a windy winter day in suburban Chicago, shopping at a Klutznick mall can be a physical challenge equal to reaching the North Pole. Later, Water Tower Place would be his crowning achievement. Again, he lived over the store (in this case Marshall Field, Lord & Taylor, and dozens of smaller shops), occupying one of the building's luxury residential units on the upper floors.

The character of these companies and the quality of the projects they developed were clearly influenced by the vocational roots of their founders—carpenters, builders, attorneys, engineers, leasing agents, supermarket managers—and the relationships they formed with major department store chains. The Simons hitched their star to Montgomery Ward, an uninspired retailer, to say the least. DeBartolo forged a great relationship with Sears, Klutznick with Marshall Field, and, again, Hahn with Broadway Stores. I was fortunate enough to earn the trust and respect of multiple national and regional department store chains, including Macy's, Sears, Marshall Field, Lord & Taylor, J. L. Hudson, Allied Stores, Saks Fifth Avenue, and promising upstarts like Kohl's and JCPenney. In fact, I built Penney's first full-line store at Southland.

Which brings me back to James O. York and our Macy's discussion. Jim was open-minded enough to hear me out.

Together, we considered the potential draw of a much larger project and a much larger store, in which Macy's would be able to present its apparel lines and soft goods in depth, fulfilling the promise of its respected brand. We drove around in the market. Jim eventually agreed with my assessment that recently built and soon-to-be-built highways were changing everything. Old shopping patterns were meaningless. Trade areas of 50,000 to 60,000 people were expanding overnight to 250,000. Without the freeways, our trade area would have encompassed a five-mile circle, in which shoppers would travel twenty minutes to the center. With the freeway, the circle expanded to ten miles, which meant three times as many people. The freeways around Sunvalley had the capacity to deliver in twenty minutes or less more than a quarter million people living within ten to fifteen miles of the center. (As we got more sophisticated, comprehensive drive-time studies and license plate surveys were conducted by our market research department to establish the size of our primary trade areas with scientific precision.)

Even though Concord and the communities surrounding it were for the most part commuter towns, the market's young families were not going to cross bridges to shop in downtown San Francisco with any regularity. And every day, more and more companies were shifting jobs out from San Francisco.

Offering two hundred shops and three or more department stores would create the critical mass to establish Sunvalley as the dominant shopping destination for this growing market. I was planning the equivalent mall shop space of two department stores (approximately 400,000 square feet), offering the same categories of goods along with around 50,000 square feet of food and services. The specialty shops would compete head-to-head with the department stores. Customers would respond to the convenience of a one-stop comparison shopping opportunity, and the area would not be splintered by multiple smaller, poorly planned retail properties. At least that was my theory.

Thank goodness Jim was convinced. And in the end, a compelling opportunity overcame entrenched threshold resistance to a new way of thinking. Jim made his positive recommendation to Macy's corporate decision makers, and Sunvalley—with a beautiful 200,000-square-foot Macy's exceeding all sales expectations—debuted in 1967 as "the world's largest air-conditioned shopping center."

Although he didn't say anything at the time, I think as we cut the ribbon at Sunvalley's grand opening Jim must have been thinking: "This better work, kid. It's *my* ass if it doesn't." Soon after, Macy's hired Jim and made him the head of its real estate department, where he enjoyed a very successful career as one of the industry's most respected executives.

The greater Bay Area turned out to be very fertile ground for the Taubman Company. In rapid succession, we built three centers there in the 1960s. The third, Eastridge, was built near San Jose, which between 1960 and 1967 saw its population soar by nearly 50 percent, making it the second-fastest-growing large metropolitan area in the country. Built on the former Hillview Golf Course, Eastridge was a 1.5-million-square-foot center with 150 stores, anchored by a large Sears, JCPenney, and May.

We took the lessons we were learning in California and applied them closer to home. In effect, we realized that by building large centers, we were essentially creating new commercial downtowns under a single roof. In 1968, we opened the Woodland Mall in Grand Rapids, Michigan. In its first full year in operation, the seventy-store mall captured 25 percent of total general merchandise sales in the Grand Rapids market.

Reimagining the size of the prospective customer base, the scale of malls, and the footprints they could occupy was an important first step in building successful, lasting retail operations. It took a lot of self-confidence and a willingness to peer deep into the future to envision the viability of our projects. To a large degree, the centers we built in the 1960s and early 1970s were bets on the construction of new highways and subdivisions. Using rental cars and gas station maps, I got very good at explaining the impact of future highways on retail locations. One adventure I remember all too well took place in the suburbs of Chicago when we were planning the development of the Woodfield mall in Schaumburg, Illinois. We were planning to spend $90 million to build a 2 million-square-foot mall in a community whose population numbered about 18,000, which required a huge leap of faith by all parties involved.

Taking a break from an industry conference in Chicago, I convinced a car full of bankers from the Chase Manhattan Bank (they had already lent us the money to buy the land) to join me for a quick drive out to the site, about twenty miles northwest of the Loop. Construction was just getting under way on the extension of Interstate 90 west of O'Hare Airport, and Woodfield was to be built on farmland right off a future exit.

I headed past the airport along small country roads, and we passed farm after farm. One looked just like the other. Hopelessly lost, I sped past a farm I thought I recognized. Waving my arm out the car window, I confidently exclaimed, "That's it!" I think the bankers knew I had no idea where we were. But they couldn't miss the signs of growth all around us. And lost or not, it was easy to grasp how Interstate 90 would dramatically shrink drive times for the families moving out to Chicago's booming northwest suburbs. An outstanding retail market was forming right before our eyes. When Woodfield opened in 1971, it was the largest enclosed mall in the country.

But situating the center in the big, macroeconomic picture was only the first step. Our centers stood out because of what happened inside their walls and in their immediate surroundings. From the outset, I believed that building shopping centers wasn't a real estate or a development business; it was a retail business. Shopping centers were department stores of stores, and we were the merchandisers. Understanding the psychology and history of retail, and understanding how properly designed stores can break down threshold resistance, gave us a competitive advantage. The real innovation we brought was the *design* of the malls.

~ FOUR ~

Evolution of the Arcade

It's common for people to view the types of malls I started build-ing in the 1960s—gigantic, air-conditioned, enclosed environ-ments—as twentieth-century American inventions. But malls are neither contemporary nor American. And while it may have seemed that I was embarking on a risky gamble, I was in fact walking in the footsteps of generations of retail pioneers.

Now, that might sound strange coming from me. Along with Victor Gruen, the Viennese architect who designed much-studied retail projects in Detroit and Minneapolis in the 1950s, I am often listed among the early creators of this "new" retail archetype. As Malcolm Gladwell, author of *The Tipping Point,* wrote in the *New Yorker,* "If Victor Gruen invented the mall, Alfred Taubman perfected it."

High praise from one of the most successful business writers of our time. But I'm going to have to decline it. Unlike Gruen, a color-ful man who embraced this questionable honor with gusto, I have never been comfortable with the accolades and blame that come with being known as one of the guys who "malled" America.

Truth is, major enclosed marketplaces with the depth of mer-chandise selection to pull customers from considerable distanc-es—otherwise known as malls—have been around for centuries.

I keep in my office a beautiful book of architectural drawings, *Monuments modernes de la Perse,* published by Pascal Coste, a French architect who studied the cities of Persia in the 1800s. It contains an illustration of a fabric bazaar in Isfahan. The shops, in this case selling spaces leased to fabric merchants, are arranged around a dramatic domed grand court with a fountain at its center. Merchandised corridors branch out from the grand court. Daylight streams in through the skylights above. Sketch in a Starbucks and you'd think you were looking at Woodfield mall.

Or consider this account written by a European traveler in 1784 describing the bazaars of Istanbul:

> Superb buildings, filled with beautiful covered passageways, most of which rest on pillars. They are all well maintained. Each business has its own hall, where the merchandise is presented . . . visitors come for entertainment as well as business.

This building type was refined in Europe, beginning almost immediately after the French Revolution, as democratic upheaval helped spawn a middle class in France eager to take on the material trappings of the upper crust. Fine apparel, home furnishings, great food, and festive entertainment were available in the arcades, of which the Galeries de Bois of the Palais Royal was perhaps the finest early example:

> One can divide the arcade into two broad categories: open arcades and covered arcades; the later being an improved version of the former.
>
> It was not enough to save the pedestrian from the distress and anxiety of the street: one had to attract him positively to the arcade so that once he entered he would feel himself caught up by its magic and forget everything else. It all depended on the ability to build an

arcade bright as an open space . . . warm in winter, and cool in summer, always dry and never dusty or dirty.

That sounds a lot like one of the Taubman Company's early leasing brochures. (By the way, experience has taught me that the quality of a real estate development is usually in inverse relation to the cost and hyperbole of its brochure!) And if your travels ever take you to Milan, make a point of visiting Galleria Vittorio Emanuele II, the quintessential mall. Opened in the 1800s, this Italian masterpiece incorporates most of the essential elements of great shopping center design on a grand scale. The mall corridors, which intersect at a domed grand court, serve as busy pedestrian passageways connecting two busy public activity centers—piazzas. The center is adjacent to the city's most active commercial and residential districts, and is anchored by a cathedral. Back when Italians attended mass far more regularly than they do today, the church acted as a "people pump" as potent as any major department store or rail station.

Explore the streets of London today, and you'll discover such thriving destinations as the Burlington Arcade, still delighting customers after more than two centuries in business. It was in fact an Englishman who brought the arcade to America. John Haviland, a British architect, designed the Philadelphia Arcade, which debuted in 1826. Additional multilevel, enclosed Haviland projects soon followed in Providence, New York, and Cleveland. Haviland died long before the introduction of Cinnabon or Victoria's Secret, but he—far more than me or Victor Gruen—really deserves the credit and the sneers for malling our great nation.

In fact, the earliest department stores were born as arcades. As individual retail tenants ran into financial difficulty, the landlord would take over the space to make sure all merchandise categories were represented sufficiently in his arcade. Over time, enough of the shops, or departments, came under the control of a single owner to merit a single name or brand for the property. Historic department stores in Europe evolved in this way, offering customers the resulting advantages of consistent return policies, predictable hours of operation, and storewide promotions.

Between the Civil War and the turn of the century, pioneering retailers in the United States like John Wanamaker in Philadelphia and Marshall Field in Chicago took advantage of the availability of machine-made goods and the dramatic growth of our cities to introduce their popular shopping emporiums. Isaac Merrit Singer's sewing machine had made it possible to mass-produce garments and shoes with a consistency (and accuracy) of size and quality never before possible. In turn, the American department store offered customers some revolutionary innovations. Because there were no longer wide variations of color, quality, and fit inherent in unique hand-made goods, items could be offered to everyone at the same price. John Wanamaker called it his "one price for all" policy. Gone were the days of bartering and haggling between buyer and seller. Money-back guarantees were honored for the first time.

Let's not forget threshold resistance. Imagine how much more confidence a shopper would have in a store that posted the same prices for all customers and was willing to take a purchase back if everything was not just right. How comforting to know that a single known and respected proprietor stood behind every sale, and that if some kid sold you the wrong size pair of shoes, the store would give you another at no charge. Finally, consider today's department stores, with their in-house boutiques and carefully delineated sectors. What are they if not vertical arcades?

So in building new centers, I was standing on the shoulders of giants. Developers and merchants for centuries had been breaking down the barriers of threshold resistance. My experiences at Sims and in Ann Arbor were helpful, but I was convinced John Wanamaker had a few things to teach me as well. We wanted to build upon the history of the arcade and tap into our nation's economic and so-cial momentum to create the most successful retail destinations ever developed.

To find the answers, I looked to America's downtowns. What were they doing right? What were they doing wrong? And how could we create the optimal retailing environment?

FIVE

Creating 100 Percent Locations

In the early 1960s, just as the first Taubman regional centers were coming on line in California, I spent some time with James Rouse at an industry conference. A mortgage broker turned urban planner, Rouse studied man's built environment and worked throughout his distinguished career to improve the quality and sensitivity of land-use decisions across the nation. While he was generally complimentary, Jim was uncertain about some of my merchandising theories. He was concerned that people would find my environments more controlling and manipulative than traditional downtown shopping districts. "You know, Al," he said, "you really can't force people to do things they don't want to do."

I certainly wasn't going to dismiss the opinion of James Rouse, who had developed thriving communities from a blank sheet of paper. But I didn't think that we were that far apart in our thinking. "Jim," I said, "many inner cities are failing, especially as retail destinations. I want to duplicate the best aspects of the downtown shopping experience and eliminate the disadvantages that are holding our cities back. Ultimately, the shopper will have more freedom to do whatever she wants in my space. That's the beauty of being able to start from scratch. By reducing the amount of threshold resistance inherent in the physical layout of traditional retail districts and focusing more on the merchandising of the space, I think both the shopper and the retailer can win. And I'm sure the landlord will be better off."

I'm not so sure I made a sale that day with James Rouse. But just consider your own experiences, and I think you'll understand my point of view.

Let's start with a typical street grid in a typical downtown. Let's say Main Street is the primary east-west commercial artery. Intersecting Main are north-south cross streets we'll name First, Second, Third, and Fourth. The distance between each cross-street along Main is about 330 feet, a typical city block. The town's most popular department store stands on the northwest corner of Main and Second. Two blocks east, at the southeast corner of Main and Fourth, is a multilevel parking deck, the primary parking spot for downtown shoppers.

Because so many shoppers park their cars at Main and Fourth, walk to the department store at Main and Second, and return to their cars, the street-front shops along Main between these two destinations are situated in what we call "100 percent" locations. They can count on the highest level of pedestrian traffic passing by their front doors day after day, and benefit the most from impulse buying. Consequently, the landlords of these buildings can command the highest retail rents. By the way, studies as far back as those conducted by Leonardo da Vinci tell us that a person feels comfortable walking only about three blocks, or 1,000 feet, from his or her home for discretionary trips. Beyond that, one senses a need to return home. That's why walkable, high-volume districts within cities are typically three blocks long.

Because of the considerable rent premium paid for direct access to pedestrian traffic, a healthy downtown typically will not feature restaurants, banks, travel agencies, and other services along Main.

These uses are less dependent upon walk-in traffic and impulse purchases, so they will be located on the cross-streets, midblock off Main. (Walk up Madison Avenue in midtown New York, one of the world's great retailing strips, and count the restaurants. You won't find many.) In struggling downtowns, as opposed to healthy ones, you tend to see those secondary uses, especially banks, occupying prime locations better suited for retail.

Now, here's where opportunities for improvement come in. In our pretend city I purposely placed the department store and parking deck on opposite sides of Main Street. In this very typical situation, a pedestrian will have to cross Main at some point between Fourth and Second on her way to the department store and back to her car. (I should point out that women are the majority of mall shoppers, and the biggest buyers of men's clothing. So when I use the word *her* or the pronoun *she,* I'm just reflecting the reality of our customer mix.)

Because of the need to cross streets, the shops on the north and south sides of Main may not get an equal shot at our customer. The busy vehicular traffic along Main stands in the way of "cross-shopping" both sides of the street. Threshold resistance in the form of a moatlike barrier of flowing cars, buses, and trucks stands in the way of the merchants' sales opportunities. Over time, this serious impediment will diminish sales significantly, leading to lower rents and lower tax revenues. It's expensive and complicated for a city to improve this situation. You could construct another parking deck a few blocks away to create more 100 percent locations. You could attract a second department store to town—if the existing department store management is not powerful enough to block it. You could close off a few blocks of Main Street to vehicular traffic. But these remedies are far from perfect; each requires millions of taxpayer dollars.

Now imagine you had a blank sheet of paper and open space relatively unencumbered by existing street grids, buildings, and political resistance. That's what we had in the 1960s with our big mall sites. We had the ability to make improvements and design a more effective shopping district. When I was interviewed by *Business Week* in 1971, I told the reporter that "with Woodfield we are not competing against other centers or suburban business districts. We are competing against downtown Chicago. So we must come as close as we can to the strength and depth of selection you find in Chicago's core area."

Like the typical downtown retail district, our plans included anchor department stores—ideally, at least two; three, four, or five is even better. We call them "anchors" because they anchor the property from both a physical and business point of view. The anchor brands defined the center in the eyes of the customer and provided the promotional impact to draw traffic. Pick up any major-market daily newspaper and you will find heavy advertising for the area's department stores. These powerful, well-defined merchants actively attract shoppers to their stores—and thus, to the mall—day in and day out. For decades, they were also the only retailers to offer credit to customers. So department stores act as "people pumps," and mall developers compete aggressively to secure their participation.

Years ago, a senior Taubman Company marketing executive asked me what I thought would be the most effective print advertisement for one of our shopping centers. Never passing up a chance to doodle, I sketched an ad with a bold headline that read, "Sale Today at Bloomingdale's."

A bit confused (and probably disappointed) the executive asked, "But, Mr. Taubman, aren't you going to mention the name of the center?" "Look closer," I said. "The center is listed as one of the Bloomingdale's locations in the New York metropolitan region. Shoppers in our trade area will see the ad and come to our Bloomingdale's. If we've done our job right, they'll be drawn into the mall, and every tenant will have the opportunity to benefit from the Bloomingdale's ad I just sketched."

The smaller tenants thrive on the traffic in the mall between the anchors, as shoppers comparison shop the center (the same way people shop the stores between the department store and parking location downtown).

In thinking about the interior design of malls, I was heavily influenced by a small but powerful book called *Townscape,* by the British architect and editor Gordon Cullen. First published in 1961, it should be required reading for every developer, architect, urban planner, and zoning official. Cullen introduced me to the importance of serial vision in planning productive, stimulating space. It's not that I didn't think about these things before reading Cullen's book. In fact, I'm cursed or blessed with what some have called "third-dimensional" or "parallax" vision. With essentially every object or vista I see, I think about how it could be better. Not just different. Better. But Cullen captured these hard-to-describe concepts in understandable, almost poetic language. Here is his paragraph on optics from the introduction to *Townscape:*

> Let us suppose that we are walking through a town: here is a straight road off which is a courtyard, at the far side of which another street leads out and bends slightly before reaching a monument. Not very unusual. We take the path and our first view is that of the street. Upon turning into the courtyard the new view is revealed instantaneously at the point of turning, and this view remains with us whilst we walk across the courtyard. Leaving the courtyard we enter the further street. Again a new view is suddenly revealed although we are traveling at a uniform speed. Finally as the road bends the monument swings into view. The significance of all this is that although the pedestrian walks through the town at a uniform speed, the scenery of towns is often revealed in a series of jerks and revelations. This we call SERIAL VISION.

Cullen explains that "a long straight road has little impact because the initial view is soon digested and becomes monotonous." He underscores the importance of what he calls "the existing view and the emerging view." And then he suggests that the experience we enjoy whenever visiting an attractive town is more than "an accidental chain of events," and argues that planners can use this understanding to create better, more stimulating environments:

> Suppose, however, that we take over this linking as a branch of the art of relationship; then we are finding a tool with which human imagination can begin to mould the city into a coherent drama. The process of manipulation has begun to turn the blind facts into a taut emotional situation.

We wanted our customer to have much the same experience Cullen describes so beautifully in *Townscape* (which is still available in a paperback version published by Architectural Press under the title *The Concise Townscape*). Again, the objective was to give every retailer a good chance of attracting the shopper into the store, to make every location a 100 percent location.

The message didn't always sink in. Years ago, I was reading a newspaper article in which one of our mall managers was asked to point out the "best location" in his center. I suppose that's a fair question for an innocent, uninitiated reporter to ask. The answer, however, was unforgivable. Our manager pointed out a location on the mall's second level near a particular department store. Now, for a particular tenant, perhaps there is a best location in one of our centers, and we work hard to determine that spot based on a whole host of variables. But to suggest that such a thing exists for a generic tenant is just short of sacrilegious! Creating 100 percent locations for all tenants is what we're all about. Counting to ten, I asked our head of operations to have a chat with the mall manager in question. I don't think he made that mistake again—at least not at one of our properties.

The key to creating 100 percent locations is moving customers effectively through our space. With inexpensive suburban land costs, it would have been cheaper (in construction expense) to spread out all the tenants on one level between potent department store anchors. But we took da Vinci's warnings to heart, and stacked the stores on two levels, creating mall corridors between the anchor department stores of around 1,000 feet, a comfortable stroll of three city blocks. We punched holes in the upper floor, allowing customers to see the stores on both levels and encouraging shopping on both sides of the corridor—retail "undulation" that would be impossible along a busy urban street. We also installed clear handrails on the upper level to preserve unobstructed sight lines, and placed vertical transportation systems (escalators and elevators) on the ends of the mall corridors to create a balanced flow of customers past every store. To test the effectiveness of these measures, at Southridge, a center we opened near Milwaukee in 1970, we gave incentives to a candy store and a hosiery store—two impulse operations—to open one store on the upper level at one end and an identical store at the lower level on the other end. We tracked each operation's sales and found that the stores ran within 4 to 5 percent of each other per month. That showed we could equalize traffic through external and internal control.

Next: parking. We surrounded the mall with convenient, close-in parking fields, free of charge. Understanding that people, like water, flow downhill much easier than uphill, we built more upper level parking (about 15 percent more than the lower-level parking areas) to assure a better balance of shopper traffic. And to reinforce that balance, we convinced the department store operator on one end of the center to reverse its traditional merchandising layout, offering the customary first-floor departments—cosmetics, jewelry, handbags—on the second level. The department store on the opposite end of the mall would merchandise in the usual manner.

Even regular visitors to Taubman malls may not notice that there are upper and lower parking lots. We graded the land to create these changes in elevation in such a way that the customer rarely thinks twice about this important balancing act. But the difference in over-all mall tenant sales is dramatic. Every space along the mall corridors becomes a 100 percent location.

To allow easy access to any parking area (our centers have no front door or back door), we designed a ring road circling the entire property. Feeding cars safely onto the ring road off major thorough-fares are what we call magazine roads—because they function much like the magazine of a gun, "loading" a number of cars for release onto the ring road. Every turn off a magazine road onto the ring road is a free right-hand turn, which allows traffic to move unimpeded.

Inside, we created an environment in which very little would stand between the customer and the merchandise. Every surface was important. For example, we determined that the flooring—the only surface the customer ever comes in contact with—was to be durable but attractive terrazzo tile patterned with regular grout joints to allow economical repair and give women with thin-soled shoes more confidence and comfort as they walked the mall. This was a dramatic improvement over a typical city's cracked sidewalks, gutters, and gratings. And to assure easy access for baby strollers and wheelchairs, our centers were built essentially barrier free.

Above, ceilings were designed of sculptured white plaster, mim-icking the effect of billowy clouds—comforting but not interesting enough to draw shoppers' eyes away from the all-important store-fronts and the merchandise. Skylights were installed to spill pools of light into the space, encouraging movement. Any perceived change in daylight by the customer tends to discourage longer stays in the mall, so we installed artificial lighting units in the skylight wells to maintain the same interior lighting levels through dusk into the eve-ning hours.

We concentrated on every human sense. There is a very distinctive sound to shopping: heels clicking, people in conversation, shopping bags in motion. Music is not necessary to set the mood. In fact, it can be negative to the experience. Scents are important, too. Hair salons and restaurants must be isolated from better dress stores and jewelry counters. To enliven the space we also incorporated court areas, punctuated by museum-quality art, into our designs at the interior entrances to department stores and in the center of the mall. James Rouse might call all this manipulation. Indeed it was. That was and is my job as a developer of retail space.

As we planned our properties, we had another important advantage over cities and towns: We could control the merchandising of the center. That's impossible when multiple landlords own the buildings in a downtown's retail district. Like a department store, we considered the most effective adjacencies for the stores. What combination of merchants made the most sense? What men's shoe store would do best adjacent to Brooks Brothers? And, years later, would shoppers appreciate a Williams-Sonoma store across from Pottery Barn?

Sounds pretty basic. But to this day, competitive mall developers lease space as if they're slicing salami. Whenever there is a vacancy, they rush to fill it with the next available tenant, oblivious to the merchandising issues and opportunities. And whenever a lease comes up for renewal, they sign the retailer up for as long as possible, no matter how tired the store. This inattention to detail penalizes the merchants, the customers, and the landlord. And in today's world of public real estate companies, it penalizes the investors.

After all, adding a tenant to a shopping center is like mixing a new element into a chemical formula. The addition changes the experience for the shopper and the merchants. That's one of the reasons the Taubman Company negotiates the *shortest* leases in the industry, averaging just five to seven years. Lease renewals always mandate store renovation, and if a retail concept has lost its appeal, we want the store out of the center—extracted from our chemical formula. In its place, we add a fresh, new concept to please shoppers and strengthen every store's opportunity.

Most observers believe that the roof on an enclosed mall is there primarily to shut out the weather. Not true in our centers. The enclosed space allows the stores to open their front doors to the customer year-round, night and day, rain or shine. Remember Milton Petrie's deep throat store design? Contrast that and all its barriers with the openness and attractiveness of a well-designed mall store like The Limited or Pottery Barn. You are almost in the store as you pass, and the merchandise calls out to you in a way it never could on the street.

When these opportunities are placed right in front of the customer (and with the assistance of knowledgeable salespeople), impulse buying increases dramatically. You run to the store for a dress shirt and end up buying two ties and a new belt. Everything other than the shirt is an impulse buy. So are the new Norah Jones CDs you pick up and the box of Godiva chocolates.

The multiplex movie theater concept was created in shopping centers to turn what was a calculated scheduling decision into more of an impulse decision. With staggered start times, cinemas can attract viewers who never intended to go to the movies when they headed to the mall. We first started putting theaters in our centers in California. The discussion of what to see shifts from the kitchen table at home to the cineplex lobby. If you've ever spontaneously found yourself in front of a movie screen holding a bag of popcorn and a large Coke, you've just made several impulse decisions. Nicely done.

This set of principles didn't emerge fully formed from my head when I started building enclosed malls in the early 1960s. But over the course of the decade, as our organization developed the experience and capabilities to develop several huge projects at once, these ideas became an integral part of our planning process. In 1970, for example, we had 7 million square feet of retail space under construction, and another 10 million in the planning stages. I was always thrilled when I found we could incorporate lessons learned from our malls in California into the design of malls we built near Milwaukee or in Grand Rapids or in the Chicago suburbs, in the late 1960s and early 1970s.

A September 1971 *Business Week* cover story focused on the burgeoning shopping center industry. Guess who appeared on the cover? Here's how they described me:

> His expensive, patent leather shoes are scuffed, and his impeccably tailored pinstripe is flecked with fresh plaster. But A. Alfred Taubman, the dapper chairman and chief executive of Taubman Co., is completely oblivious to it all. He is lost somewhere up there in the soaring scaffolds, where workers are busily putting the final touches to Woodfield.

Dapper? That's about the nicest thing any reporter has ever said about me. But I can't believe my shoes were scuffed. The article goes on to capture the passion I felt for my centers then and still do now:

> "Just look at this!" the bouncy, 47-year-old developer marvels to a visitor. "Fantastic! Imagine all the logistics and planning that have to go into something like this. Boy," he sighs, "you gotta be a little nuts."

I've been called much worse. But you get the idea. Planning is everything. Screw that up, and a retail development will never realize its fullest potential. Get it right and everybody wins.

While we spoke many times after our discussion at that industry conference in the early 1960s, I never struck up a close personal relationship with James Rouse. Judging from the design of his later enclosed centers, however, I think he did come over a bit to my way of thinking. And our retail properties flourished, as retailers embraced our properties as launching pads for exciting new concepts and unprecedented growth.

For the Taubman Company, too, horizons never looked brighter.

SIX

Buying the Ranch

Selecting the correct sites and designing and merchandising the malls properly were certainly instrumental to our early success. But without the proper financial architecture, none of these projects would have succeeded. I wasn't a numbers person by training, and I was never the type of developer who felt that it was crucial to pinch pennies at every stage of the operation. Again, it was design that mattered most. If the financing and leases were structured in the right way, and the incentives of the landlord and the tenant were properly aligned, I knew we'd do fine financially in the long run.

Here, too, we made some innovations. I was fortunate to work with responsive lenders. TIAA, the big insurance company, financed many of my early projects. When we were about to close on a $20 million mortgage on the Sunvalley mall, they called the day before closing and said they couldn't close until the following day because their check-writing machines handled only seven digits. So they went out and bought a new one.

When we started building, the process was as follows: a developer would design a center, sign up some early leases, and get a mortgage commitment. The mortgage commitment stipulated that if the developer met targets for opening dates and the number of AAA-rated tenants, then the lender would lend a certain amount against the property. Then the developer would get a bank to lend against that commitment so the center could be built. This process seemed to have it backward, since it encouraged developers to sign up tenants early in the process. To me, the best tenants are the ones you get toward the end of the leasing process, when you have something real to show them. Ultimately, I went to Chase and convinced them that they should give me a commitment to build, and that I'd start leasing once the space was built.

We took great care in selecting retailers, starting with the anchors. The long-term agreements entered into between department store companies and retail developers determine to a large extent the value of the shopping center. These complex contracts are called "covenants of operation" and "reciprocal easement agreements." That's legal terminology for mutually establishing hours of operation, shared costs, and most important of all, the quality and character of the department store that will do business at the property for a set term. In other words, if Saks Fifth Avenue agrees to be part of the shopping center for twenty years, the company assures the developer that a Saks store or another of the same quality and character will anchor the mall—and help draw customers—for two decades to come.

Against that promise (and the promises of the other anchor stores in the project), the developer can lease the mall tenant space at attractive rents. Specialty stores want a shot at the Saks customer and are willing to pay for that opportunity. Here, again, we innovated. Most developers charged fixed rent that was based on their costs of land, construction, and operation. But I didn't see myself as a landlord renting spaces to tenants. I saw myself as a retailer with an ongoing business. So in our centers, we structured our leases based on the gross volume of retailers. They would pay a fixed rent plus a percentage of sales above a certain level. That had the effect of aligning our interests. If I could figure out how to bring more people to the centers, and design the centers in such a way as to increase impulse purchases, we'd both win. That's one of the reasons we became so good at promoting our centers: we saw that as part of our job. In 1974, we brought the Chicago Symphony Orchestra to Woodfield, and it drew an audience of 30,000. The music lovers came for the brass and the woodwinds, but a lot of them stayed to shop.

In thinking about promotion, retailers and developers are well-advised to take cues from other industries. I learned a great deal from my buddy Warner LeRoy, son of the legendary MGM movie director-producer Mervyn LeRoy (his impressive credits included such major pictures as *The Wizard of Oz*). Warner came into the public eye in the late 1960s when he opened the hotter-than-hot Manhattan nightspot Maxwell's Plum (where Donald Trump met his first wife, Ivana). His next triumph was Tavern on the Green, which captured his personal flare for theater and quality. Toward the end of his life, he acquired the aging Russian Tea Room, into which he poured his heart and soul. Warner knew how to create a buzz and sustain public interest. And the stories he told about growing up on the sound stages of early Hollywood could hold your undivided attention for hours.

As counterintuitive as it may seem, we always tried to open with empty stores. Our centers were planned initially to open with at least 15 percent vacancy through the end of their first full year of operation. That gave us an opportunity to see what types of stores had the greatest appeal in the market and figure out what we were missing before we fully committed our space. Remember, a center is like a big store. We wanted to see which goods moved and which didn't. To me, anytime a center opens 100 percent leased, it's a real estate failure. I always saw myself as being in business with our tenants, not as being in an adversarial relationship with them. Indeed, over the years, I formed close personal and business relationships with many of my tenants. One was Les Wexner, founder of The Limited and a true retailing genius. In the mid-1970s, I took Les on a helicopter ride to see our Detroit-area centers, Fairlane Town Center, Lakeside, and Twelve Oaks. Each had a Limited store.

Wexner was a natural merchant. At that time, his stores, in my opinion, were not designed to maximize the opportunity of an enclosed regional mall location. His merchandise was right on target, but the stores essentially turned their back on the mall and the customer. They looked like warehouses, with racks hung on strips on the wall. "Les," I said, "your stores are a blight on my shopping centers." I told him that he had to redesign the stores or we would not have The Limited in our centers. Fortunately, he agreed with my analysis. Our company's store planning and design department lent a hand, and today, all divisions of The Limited and its spin-off brands, which certainly no longer need our help, are among the most successful stores in any mall: open, inviting, and full of energy. And Les Wexner has become one of my dearest friends—and a great patron of fine architecture.

In two decades working as a builder and developer, I had been fortunate to form many long-lasting personal and professional relationships. Doing business with the same people over time builds trust and can lead to terrific opportunities. Over the years, I joined corporate boards, invested in other businesses, and continually built a network of contacts and colleagues.

Not all of these opportunities were attractive. In the 1970s, I was invited to Iran by the shah and his wife to consider development of a U.S.-style shopping center on the main highway from Tehran to the airport. I passed on the offer when I learned that essentially the entire ruling family and its chief advisers and ministers lived in and conducted business out of Geneva, Switzerland. I'm glad I followed my instincts. The threshold resistance was way too high.

Some long-standing contacts, however, allowed me to apply my theories of threshold resistance to real estate investing in a more hospitable climate. The opportunity came about in large part because of relationships I had formed working in California. In the late 1950s, I had first met Jimmy Peters. At the time, Jimmy and his brothers Leone and Tony were running the prospering New York real estate brokerage firm of Cushman & Wakefield. Jimmy introduced me to Charles Allen Jr., a very successful New York banker and a great businessman. Charles and his brother, Herb, were my partners in our earliest West Coast shopping centers. To return the favor, I introduced Jimmy to Warren Sconing, head of real estate for Sears. They hit it off, and Cushman ended up handling the Sears Tower. I also brought Jimmy to Detroit to make a deal with Detroit Bank and Trust (now Comerica) on their headquarters building on Fort Street. These were Cushman & Wakefield's first major assignments outside New York.

One day in 1976, Charles Allen called to ask me if I was familiar with the Irvine Ranch. He wanted me to go take a look at it because he thought we had an opportunity to buy it.

The Irvine Ranch—77,000 acres of prized property in Southern California's Orange County—was one of the most beautiful master-planned communities in the nation, and it had a storied past.

James Irvine, born in Belfast, Ireland, in 1827, came to America in 1846. He worked for a couple of years in a New York paper mill before heading to California in search of gold. Instead, he found riches in land. James became a successful produce merchant in San Francisco and began investing in real estate. By 1864, he had done well enough to join with two partners in purchasing three huge Mexican and Spanish land grants—Rancho San Joaquin, Rancho Lomas de Santiago, and a portion of Rancho Santiago de Santa Ana—which at the time covered 120,000 acres along the Pacific Ocean south of Los Angeles. James gradually bought out his partners and used the land primarily for sheep grazing. Irvine's holdings gained in value as the

Southern Pacific and Santa Fe railroads were completed to Los Angeles in the 1870s and 1880s. He died in 1886, just as new residents began flocking to Southern California to start new lives.

The provisions of his will gave control of the ranch to his son, James Irvine II, when he turned twenty-five, in 1893. (It is reported that the young man, known as J.I., first traveled at age eighteen from San Francisco to San Diego on a high-wheeled bicycle to see his father's holdings.) J.I. shifted the business focus of the ranch from sheep and cattle raising to agriculture, making land available for tenant farming (mostly hay and grain). In 1894, he incorporated his holdings as the Irvine Company under the laws of West Virginia, one of only a few states that allowed corporations at the time.

When sophisticated irrigation systems were developed throughout the first decades of the new century, J.I. turned his attention to the very profitable citrus industry. The same speedy, dependable rail lines delivering settlers to Southern California made it possible to ship fresh produce affordably across the continent. The land was soon covered with walnut, orange, and lemon trees, with vegetable fields, and irrigation systems.

Under the direction of J.I.'s son, James Irvine III, the ranch became one of the largest landholdings under cultivation in the United States, boasting the finest asparagus crop and Valencia orange groves in the world.

For estate planning purposes and to fund educational and charitable projects in Orange County and San Francisco, J.I. in 1937 established the James Irvine Foundation, which held his controlling interest in the Irvine Company. Upon his death, in 1947 (he apparently drowned while fishing in a stream on a Montana cattle ranch owned by the Irvine Company), his stock passed to the foundation as trustee on behalf of the people of California. J.I.'s only living son, Myford Irvine, served as president of the Irvine Company until his mysterious death in 1959. Apparently, Myford was not very well liked. He was found dead in the basement of his home with multiple gunshot wounds (two in the stomach from a 16-gauge shotgun and one in the head from a .22-caliber revolver). The official cause of death was determined to be "suicide."

Throughout the decade that followed, Joan Irvine Smith, J.I.'s granddaughter, acted as a much-needed watchdog for the family, as foundation trustees sought to benefit personally from the rich resources of the ranch. Joan also pushed for innovative land-use planning and donated 1,000 acres for the development of the University of California, Irvine, campus. Thanks in large measure to Joan's personal lobbying, federal and state laws were amended in 1969 to limit the percentage of ownership a foundation may hold in a corporation to just 20 percent. The new regulations gave foundations twenty years to meet this restriction. But rather than sell off portions of their stock over time, the trustees of the James Irvine Foundation pursued a sale of all their holdings in the ranch. Trustee Simon Fluor—whose company had an active relationship with Mobil Oil—brokered a sale of the foundation's controlling interest in the ranch to Mobil. When she learned of the pending transaction by accident, Joan Irvine Smith in December 1974 filed suit in California to stop the deal. The California state attorney general, agreeing that the offer was too low and the sale procedure was flawed, joined Mrs. Smith in her action. Intense legal wrangling ensued for the next two years.

In August 1976, I got the fateful call from my partner Charles Allen Jr.

He suggested that I go down to Beverly Hills to meet with a Colonel Gotleib, a lifelong friend of Allen's, who would introduce me to Joan Irvine Smith, the largest Irvine Company shareholder other than the foundation, and Keith Gaede, the husband of Joan's cousin. At the time I certainly was aware of the Irvine Ranch, which covered about 22 percent of the land area of booming Orange County (at the time home to about 1.5 million people), stretching more than twenty miles inland from the coast. I had also long admired Irvine's state-of-the-art master plan, and had been following Mobil's battle to acquire the company. I flew into Orange County Airport the next day.

I was impressed with Joan Smith the minute I met her. You could sense her determination and love for the ranch. It was also clear that she was one tough woman. I later learned that she had divorced her first husband after discovering that he was having an affair. The story goes that when Joan learned of her unfaithful husband's rendezvous with his girlfriend at Joan's horse ranch in Virginia, she had the place surrounded by security personnel and threatened to burn the house down.

But before I could endorse a bid higher than Mobil's $24-per-share offer, I needed to make the proper appraisal and evaluation. That could take weeks, even on a fast track. Smith assured me that the company's records would be open for our review, and promised that management would be available to answer our questions. We put together a team of Taubman Company personnel headed by Bob Schout, our head of market research, assembled our outside consultants, and went to work.

When we completed our initial appraisal in late September, it was clear to us that Mobil was trying to buy the company on the cheap. Now, it may have seemed the height of folly for a guy from Detroit to start a bidding war against a huge multinational oil company. But I sensed that our team had an advantage. By nature and temperament, we could look at this asset—and its potential—in a fundamentally different light. Where we saw it as a real estate deal, Mobil, an industrial company, was going to operate the ranch as an industrial business. I also was sure they were assessing the value of the company using their conventional corporate earnings-per-share basis. After all, they had acquired other companies based on this type of analysis.

Here's how Mobil probably saw it. The Irvine Company had

earned approximately $10.9 million after taxes in fiscal 1974–75; it was not out of line to offer nineteen to twenty times earnings, or about $218 million for the 8.4 million shares outstanding. Their offer on the table when we got interested was $24 per share, or $192 million. The Irvine Company's earnings had been growing at about 10–12 percent annually, which gave Mobil confidence that the deal would contribute to their own financial results. Clearly, they had room to go higher.

But how high were we willing to go? We looked beyond earnings per share and appraised the value of the opportunity on the basis of land value and real estate development upside, which led to a significantly higher present-day valuation: at least $400 million. If we played our cards right, we could outbid Mobil and still get the ranch at a huge discount to its value. We opened our bidding at $27 per share, $3 more than Mobil's offer. The courts recognized our offer and opened the bidding.

This deal got started because of prior relationships, and it moved forward because of them, too. Wells Fargo had been our lead bank on the West Coast for nineteen years, and we had developed an excellent relationship. I thought they would be the perfect catalyst to bring together a consortium of banks to finance what would be one of the largest real estate transactions in history. In October, Wells Fargo committed to be our lead bank. In November, I added my good friend Ben Lambert of Eastdil Realty to the team to assist with the structuring of a preliminary business plan and land absorption projections to present to the banks. I also brought on Kenneth Leventhal to handle accounting matters after Ken and his associate, Stan Ross, came all the way from Los Angeles to my office in Detroit and made an impressive presentation and an impassioned plea for the business. In concluding his pitch, Ken remarked, "Mr. Taubman, if we don't get the assignment to work with you on the Irvine Ranch, I intend to slit my wrists!" That's dedication.

In the meantime, the bidding intensified when the Canadian real estate firm, Cadillac Fairview Corporation, offered $265 million in the form of cash and notes—notes guaranteed by the pledging of Irvine Ranch ground leases.

Determining that the Irvine Company on a present-value basis was worth at least $50 per share, we upped our offer to $31.81 per share. Charles Allen and I also felt it would be wise to bring in additional partners.

The first person I called was Max Fisher, my dear friend from Detroit whose financial resources were matched by his extraordinary business judgment. My next calls were to other close friends: Henry Ford II, chairman of the Ford Motor Company, and Howard Marguleas, a nationally known agriculturist with many years of farming experience throughout California. I had developed a close personal relationship with Henry in Detroit, and Max and I had worked with Howard as fellow members of the United Brands board of directors. We also included Milton Petrie and were joined by Joan Irvine Smith. To round out the group, we included Donald Bren, one of the leading land developers in California. Don had constructed thousands of housing units in the state, many of which were developed on the Irvine Ranch. Each of these partners brought much-needed expertise as well as financial resources to our team. We also liked and trusted one another.

While Cadillac Fairview and our new Taubman-Allen-Irvine team continued the bidding process, we conducted personal meetings with the eight additional banks selected to round out our consortium. In addition to Wells Fargo, we were joined by Chase Manhattan Bank of New York, First National Bank of Boston, the Bank of New York, Security Pacific, Seattle First National, Citibank of New York, Bank of America, and Manufacturers National Bank of Detroit. (I was now a board member of the bank that had provided my $5,000 loan in 1950 to start the Taubman Company.)

Cadillac Fairview dropped out of the bidding in April 1977, which allowed us to focus exclusively on Mobil. Under court supervision, the bidding continued on a day-to-day basis. Each party was allowed just twenty-four hours to outbid the opposition. All bids were to be cash or its equivalent only. On May 2, Mobil opened with a bid of $36.50 per share.

My partners had granted me the authority to bid up to $400 million on behalf of the shareholders, who had agreed to capitalize Taubman-Allen-Irvine personally for not less than $100 million. We would borrow the remaining $300 million.

It is important to note that our analysis of a present-value purchase of $400 million was based on future-value assets in excess of $600 million. Unlike bureaucratic Mobil Oil, we evaluated the Irvine Company as a real estate investment, based on real estate assets. We also recognized the value of the more than $100 million in road and utility infrastructure already in the ground, waiting for development.

In addition, the hundreds of residential ground leases held by such millionaire homeowners as advertising guru David Ogilvy represented a large asset. The ability to raise these lease payments substantially over time would boost revenue, and we predicted that most residents would opt to purchase the land under their homes rather than pay the escalating rents. My good friends Claude Ballard of Goldman Sachs and Shire Rothbart of the Taubman Company were heavily involved in assessing and ultimately following through on this extraordinary refinancing opportunity.

In negotiating anything, it is essential that you clearly establish your own objectives and point of view. It also helps to understand just where the other party is coming from. The Irvine Company's reported corporate earnings were incidental to our basic evaluation model. But they were critical to Mobil. We predicted, based on Irvine Company 1976 year-end earnings of $17.9 million, that the maximum bidding authority granted by Mobil's board would be approximately nineteen times earnings, or $340 million. We were betting Mobil would quit before reaching that ceiling.

On May 9 we outbid Mobil by $0.25, bringing our offer to $309.25 million.

Mobil countered on May 10 at $37.60 per share, or $316.4 million.

The next day we returned the compliment at $37.75, or $317.66 million.

They countered on May 12 at $38.25, or $321.87 million.

We came back with $38.35 per share on the thirteenth for $322.7 million.

I will always remember fondly the daily phone calls with my sons, Bobby and Billy, during this manic, high-stakes bidding war. They would always want me to counter Mobil's offer, and would encourage me with a spirited mix of well-thought-out rationale and youthful optimism (Bobby was twenty-four, Billy just nineteen). Their competitive juices were flowing, and so were mine.

After a tense weekend, Mobil bid $38.75 per share, or $326.1 million.

We came right back the next day at $39 per share, or $328.185 million.

Mobil's president, who was handling the bidding personally, gave us his full and last shot on May 18 at $40 per share, or $336.6 million.

My small bump of $0.10 to $40.10, or $337.44, ended the bidding on May 19. We were notified the next day that Mobil had withdrawn—just $3 million below the ceiling I predicted.

By the aggressive terms of our offering agreement, we had only two months to complete this massive deal. So after a full-court press by all our banks and associates, we met in the Los Angeles offices of Wells Fargo for the closing on July 22, 1977. I had never seen so many lawyers, bankers, and boxes of documents in one room in my life. Unfortunately, the champagne would have to wait.

Charlie Johnson of Wells Fargo pulled me into a small private room and informed me that there was an unexpected snag. Some years earlier, Don Bren had sold his company to International Paper, which had wanted a presence in the Southern California real estate industry. Things didn't go as anticipated, so Don bought back his company, granting International Paper certain warrants to buy back in if they wished.

Don was a partner in Taubman-Allen-Irvine as an individual. But the clever folks at IP wanted Bren's company, in which they still had the right to 50 percent ownership, to hold the interest in the ranch, thus setting up the opportunity for IP to get into the deal. They were holding up the assets Bren had pledged for our deal without their blessing.

While we waited in that crowded board room in Los Angeles, Wells Fargo representatives in New York were frantically trying to work something out with International Paper and Bren's lender, Bank of America, to no avail. Sensing that we were at an impasse, Charlie proposed plan B. Wells Fargo would extend me the credit for Don Bren's portion of the equity. That would allow us to close on schedule. It would be up to me to collect from Don and let him back into the deal or hang onto the larger ownership stake myself. I agreed to plan B. At the very last minute, Bren worked out a $5 million payment to IP, and we began the hours-long process of signing documents and shaking hands. The closing then went forward without a hitch.

Despite these annoyances, things worked out very well for us. Without selling any assets, we paid off the banks in fifty-one weeks! I served as the chairman of the Irvine Company, which we incorporated as a Michigan company, for six years. The company's performance exceeded our most ambitious expectations, paying out 20 percent dividends to the shareholders annually.

Delighted with our returns and recognizing that intense local management was required to sustain this success, my partners and I (not including the Irvine family members) decided to sell our interests in the company in 1983 to Don Bren. The transaction was based on a valuation of $1 billion. Don continues to ably run the company to this day.

A billion dollars was a lot of money in 1983. And who wouldn't be happy with a tenfold profit in six years, on top of the 20 percent annual dividends we paid out? I certainly can't complain, but I have to be honest. I really didn't want to sell the ranch.

In 1983, I was still in my fifties and running my businesses with more focus and energy than ever. I also saw continued upside potential for the Irvine Company. On the other hand, my close friends and partners Henry Ford II, Max Fisher, and Milton Petrie were in their late sixties and seventies, and for the most part had retired from active business lives. From their point of view, cashing out made all the sense in the world. One very important aspect of being a good partner is respecting the wishes of your fellow partners, even if they are not perfectly aligned with yours.

So we sold the ranch and almost never looked back. And as I continued to build centers and develop projects, I also pursued other investment opportunities.

SEVEN

A Frosted Mug of Root Beer

If you are younger than forty, you probably can't remember a time in America before interstate highways. So you surely never experienced the joy of crowding into your family's unreliable, unairconditioned car to bump along secondary roads to a vacation destination or relative's home. There was one aspect of these long-forgotten journeys that I always looked forward to. Often, in the most unpredictable places, you came upon a family-owned diner that offered classic American culinary delights: delicious hash browns, hamburgers, hot dogs, homemade pies, and milk shakes. The food was so good, you didn't even notice the filthy washrooms, surly waitresses, sticky counters, and busted jukeboxes. Then again, you could be equally disappointed with a restaurant chosen entirely by the persuasiveness of faded billboards or the cycles of grandma's bladder. And those unfortunate stops kept on disappointing for miles and miles, often requiring a number of urgent unplanned visits to the nasty restrooms of gas stations down the road.

Pardon the pun, but dining along the highways of America in the 1940s and 1950s was a crapshoot. That is, until the orange-roofed outposts of Howard Johnson's popped up all over the country along two-lane highways. A meal at HoJo's never delighted anybody, although those fried clams were something special. But a family making the trek from Grand Rapids to Cleveland or from Pittsburgh to Miami, could pull into any Howard Johnson's parking lot with confidence that the restrooms would be reasonably clean and the food would be less than life threatening. Everything was consistent and controlled, from the waitresses' uniforms to the taste of the HoJo Cola (no Coke or Pepsi sold here).

America's first franchise motel company, Holiday Inn, was founded in the early 1950s by Memphis home builder Kemmons Wilson with much the same promise. You never wrote home about the accommodations, but every Holiday Inn met certain standards of cleanliness and service, regardless of its location. Pull in with your weary family after a day of dusty driving, and you knew just what to expect.

I call this type of consumer promise *consistent mediocrity*. Don't underestimate its power, especially at lower price points. Howard Johnson restaurants and Holiday Inn motels had the same underlying appeal that food giants such as McDonald's, Burger King, and Wendy's have. Are you passionately drawn to the sandwich you order at Wendy's, or are you more interested in its competitive price, consistency, and convenience? McDonald's rarely comes out on top in newspaper surveys of the best burgers in town. America's quick-serve burger franchises, now doing successful business around the world, are really in the frozen food distribution business. They specialize in serving customers a protein fix in environments of little excitement or delight. But a Quarter Pounder with cheese tastes the same in Baltimore or Beijing. And McDonald's bathrooms are clean all over the planet—no small feat!

Consistent mediocrity is the quick-serve franchise's most important brand promise. And that's where I saw an opportunity.

In the 1970s, Max Fisher, the Milstein brothers, Carl Lindner (chairman of Great American Insurance in Cincinnati), and I owned

52 percent of United Brands, the produce giant known for such international food brands as Chiquita Bananas and John Morell Meats. (It was a great investment for us—we bought in at $4.25 per share and sold at $26.) One of our companies was A&W Restaurants, the first franchise food operation in the world. In 1922, two California entrepreneurs named Roy Allen and Frank Wright created a "healthy herb drink" they called root beer. From their first barrel-shaped root beer stand, Allen and Wright introduced distinctive drive-in restaurants and stands along America's highways. Unlike Howard Johnson's or McDonald's, however, the environment of a typical A&W—complete with waitresses on roller skates—was exciting. The company's frosted mugs of fresh root beer were special.

United Brands research found that consumers familiar with A&W had far deeper, and more positive, emotional ties to the brand than they did to McDonald's or any other fast-food franchise. People equated A&W with first dates, graduation celebrations, and memorable family outings. And they loved the taste of the root beer and root beer floats, especially when served in a heavy glass mug right out of the freezer. (Always put the ice cream in the mug first, and then pour in the root beer to avoid overflowing.)

Unfortunately, A&W had grown out of control. No two of the company's 2,000 units looked alike. Operators had negotiated their own deals, closing down for the winter months and buying few, if any, supplies through the company's Santa Monica, California, headquarters. With consumers losing confidence and the brand losing its distinctiveness, United Brands decided in the early 1980s to divest the A&W Restaurants business along with the rights to all on-premises serving of A&W Root Beer. (The bottling and canning rights to the beverage were sold separately.)

Convinced that the franchise still had plenty of magic, I bought A&W Restaurants from United Brands in 1982 for a relative pittance: $4 million. It was no Irvine Ranch, but the challenge and opportunity really interested me. In the year or so before my acquisition, A&W had begun to test new-concept A&W Great Food Restaurant units, which featured broader menus including salad bars, homemade ice cream, fresh hamburgers (never frozen), and all-beef hot dogs. Several of the prototypes had set up shop in our malls and were flourishing.

A shopping center's food offerings are very important. Attractive sit-down or "tablecloth" restaurants hold the customer longer in the mall and increase the number of monthly visits. With such popular national chains as P. F. Chang's China Bistro, California Pizza Kitchen, Brio Tuscan Grille, and the Cheesecake Factory well represented in today's better mall properties, it's hard to believe there was a time when it was nearly impossible to convince good restaurant operators to locate in regional shopping centers. But that certainly was the case. The earliest malls in America stayed open only two evenings a week, following the traditional schedules of their anchor department stores. No restaurant could make it on lunches and afternoon walk-in traffic alone.

Once again, we went against the grain. From the opening of our very first projects (after overcoming intense community and union opposition), Taubman centers featured extended business hours— 10 a.m. to 9 or 10 p.m. Monday through Saturday, and noon to 5 p.m. on Sundays. With great traffic and longer hours, restaurant operators began to take a look. But strict labor laws and union regulations made it difficult for establishments employing more than a few people to make ends meet.

Largely to overcome these challenges, we developed the very first food court at Southland Mall in Hayward, California, in 1964. World's Fare, as we called it, featured eight to ten kitchens offering a variety of food choices from Chinese and Italian to burgers and pizza. Tables for all the restaurants were located in a common court policed by mall personnel. Everything was served on china, which was cleaned in a central dishwashing facility. The World's Fare establishments—smaller operations than typical full-service restaurants—were owned by individual families, thus solving the labor problems and allowing for very economical delivery of good food. Mom and dad, brothers and sisters, aunts and uncles could work morning, noon, and night, without violating any regulations, to keep their businesses prospering. These were some of the most dedicated, hardworking people I have ever met. And the customers loved the opportunity for each member of their family to select a favorite cuisine. Service was fast, the setting was comfortable, and shoppers could resume their shopping relaxed and refreshed.

The new A&W Great Food Restaurant concept was demonstrating just how appealing an antidote to consistent mediocrity could be. Sales were terrific in our mall-based stores. To help deliver on our fresh food promise, we had a full-time dietitian on staff. With her help we introduced whole wheat buns for our hamburgers (our meat was never frozen in the Great Food restaurant), posted the calorie count for all items on our colorful menu boards, and tested a variety of new offerings, ranging from chili burgers to salads with low-fat dressings.

In short order we closed about 1,500 of the 2,000 A&W units (that many were underperforming or just doing their own thing) and began building franchise-owned Great Food and traditional restaurants. We reworked the remaining franchise agreements and designed affordable renovation packages to assure more quality and consistency throughout the chain. In a few years, the number of stores climbed back up to around seven hundred. Special attention was paid to our very successful restaurants in the Asia Pacific markets, especially the Philippines and Indonesia. Interestingly, root beer is a taste enjoyed in most parts of the world except Great Britain. There, it seems, the most popular toothpaste brand tastes just like root beer. (That's a level of threshold resistance not even the most clever marketer could overcome.)

I took a personal interest in the quality of our hot dogs. I consider myself a connoisseur when it comes to sausage, and hot dogs are in the sausage family of foods. The best sausage in the world, at least in my opinion, is produced in Hungary. So, shortly after acquiring A&W, I visited several *Wurstmackers* (sausage makers) in Budapest to see what I could learn. After they realized I was a good customer, a few of the more friendly wurstmackers shared their secrets. One tip kept coming up in all my conversations: garlic was the critical ingredient. They also agreed that the best all-beef sausage should be made of chuck or shoulder meat, a more flavorful cut that gave the hot dog more texture and bite.

Armed with the knowledge of the masters, I returned to the United States—Queens, New York, to be specific—to find a manufacturer willing and able to produce the best all-beef hot dog in the world. After much trial and error, we came up with the perfect recipe, full of taste, lower in fat, with just a hint of garlic. Our A&W quarter-pound hot dogs—always steamed first, then rolled on a grill—were a big hit. I would send dozens of them to my friends all over the world. We also sold these delicious hot dogs to country clubs, where they were included on the menu as "steak dogs."

You might be wondering if flying off to Budapest to meet with sausage gurus is the best use of an entrepreneur's time. You bet it is. Your product is all-important. Why should your customer be excited about your business and its offerings if you're not? Ralph Waldo Emerson famously observed that "there is no strong performance without a little fanaticism in the performer." Right on. Nothing pleases me more than to learn that a customer and his or her family have had a great experience in one of our malls. It doesn't matter if you are selling a $40,000 automobile or a $2 hot dog. Customers know if they are receiving value, and they will reward you with their loyalty whenever they do so. And once we got the hot dog perfected, I knew people would find special value and enjoyment in a visit to A&W Restaurants.

Of course, not all my creative efforts to redefine and reenergize A&W were successful. In fact, one experience in particular still leaves a very bad taste in my mouth. We were aggressively marketing a one-third-pound hamburger for the same price as a McDonald's Quarter Pounder. But despite our best efforts, including first-rate TV and radio promotional spots, they just weren't selling. Perplexed, we called in the renowned market research firm Yankelovich, Skelly, and White to conduct focus groups and competitive taste tests.

Well, it turned out that customers preferred the taste of our fresh beef over traditional fast-food hockey pucks. Hands down, we had a better product. But there was a serious problem. More than half of the participants in the Yankelovich focus groups questioned the price of our burger. "Why," they asked, "should we pay the same amount for a third of a pound of meat as we do for a quarter-pound of meat at McDonald's? You're overcharging us." Honestly. People thought a third of a pound was less than a quarter of a pound. After all, three is less than four!

We tried a half-pound burger (two patties to the pound) for just ten cents more than a Quarter Pounder. That wasn't a big hit either.

Needless to say, I was depressed by this experience, enough so, that I started to get more involved in K–12 education, teacher training, and public school reform. There is an important lesson to be learned from all this. Sometimes the messages we send to our customers through marketing and sales information are not as clear and compelling as we think they are. A product benefit you value may not be high on the list of the consumer's needs. Research is worth the cost, especially if you are investing millions of dollars in an advertising campaign that could confuse more than convince. The customer is always right, even if he or she never mastered fractions!

We also came to another important conclusion. While working hard to differentiate A&W Restaurants from the frozen-food emporiums like McDonald's, it didn't help to focus our marketing on a direct comparison with these competitors. That just reinforced the notion that we were one of them. By naming our product a "third-pounder," we framed our offering within the context of the powerful McDonald's Quarter Pounder. That diminished the more important messages of fresh beef, healthy menu choices, and frosted mugs of the best root beer in the world.

When we found the right buyer, in 1994, we sold A&W Restaurants for nearly $20 million. We had righted the ship, rekindled the magic, developed a terrific food tenant for our centers, and created a franchise organization equipped to nurture a venerable brand. The only thing I regret is that I didn't buy the bottling and canning rights to A&W Root Beer. United Brands offered them to me for around $35 million at the time I acquired the restaurants. A few years later they were sold to a Texas venture capital company for $135 million. Of course, at the time, I didn't see how the root beer would help my shopping center business. The restaurants could and did.

But from this experience I can attest that restaurateurs really do have to live over the store. With an increasing array of investment interests to watch over, I left it to others to get the garlic just right.

– EIGHT –

Minding the Store

In the early 1980s, our two malls in the Washington, D.C., area—Lakeforest in Gaithersburg, Maryland, and Fair Oaks in Fairfax, Virginia—were anchored by Woodward & Lothrop department stores. Woodies, as it was affectionately called, was the strongest regional department store chain with the best locations in arguably the best retail market in the country. Since its founding, in 1873, by Samuel Walter Woodward and Alvin Mason Lothrop, Woodies had earned its reputation as the most trusted retailer in the nation's capital.

Now, for as long as I can remember, critics have described department stores like Woodies as dinosaurs. Going back to the 1950s, it has been hard to find a vocal champion of this much-maligned institution. The same cocktail party philosophers who express knee-jerk disdain for suburbs, malls, and developers, universally rail against department stores—usually while dressed from head to toe in evening apparel purchased at one of the emporiums they slander.

To be sure, many department store chains have deserved the fate of the dinosaurs. But it's too easy to dismiss the contributions and continuing relevance of what I believe was the most important retailing institution of the twentieth century. Every good retailer understands that the customer, God love her, lacks confidence. (Again, please excuse the "her." I am just reflecting the fact that the vast majority of mall and department store customers are women. And for the record, male customers lack confidence, too.) While this inherent insecurity contributes to threshold resistance, it also presents the good retailer with a golden opportunity. By earning the trust and confidence of your shoppers—through product knowledge, service, taste level, and consistency—you can win a customer's loyalty for life. Purchasing a dress or a pair of shoes is a far more enjoyable experience if you are guided and supported in your decisions by a professional, courteous salesperson who wants to help you look your best. And it's even better if the store in which you are buying the apparel stands for something important to you and meshes with your self-image.

In other words, a clearly defined brand bolsters a customer's confidence. So does a good salesperson. And no selling institution or product distribution system in history has combined the power of branding and salesmanship better than the department store. Pioneering American department store merchants like Marshall Field and John Wanamaker, as previously noted, used mass production and product standardization to offer customers unprecedented levels of selection and value. They also built sufficient critical mass into their organizations to create buying power (holding prices down) and promotional impact. Urban newspaper readers learned about sales at downtown department stores every day. Seasonal sales and special events drew people into town from far and wide. Artfully designed store windows featured the fashions of the day and set styles for everyone to follow. Colorful shopping bags adorned with department store logos were seen in the hands of beautiful people all over town.

I thought I knew something about department stores. I served on the board of Macy's from 1986 to 1995. I also helped create a national platform—the regional mall—where department stores competed with agile specialty stores. And I believed Woodies had some competitive advantages in its excellent Washington home market.

After all, through the ups and downs of the economy, our federal government keeps cranking, supporting a well-paid, stable workforce in which women are well represented. Elections every two years create positive population turnover. The working women of Washington (coming to D.C. from cities all over America) were eager to fit in with the city's distinctive sartorial style. They trusted Woodward & Lothrop to outfit them with just the right professional, casual, and special occasion wardrobe.

The chairman of Woodies at the time was a highly respected merchant and businessman named Edwin Hoffman. Working through the Lakeforest and Fair Oaks deals, Ed and I had become good friends. We spent enough time on golf courses together (Ed belonged to several of the best country clubs on the East Coast) and at a few University of Michigan football games to really understand and trust each other. After decades of dedicated but sleepy management by members of the Woodward and Lothrop families, Ed had clearly kicked some new life into Woodies, then the nation's largest independent publicly traded department store chain. In 1983, sales in Woodies' seventeen Washington-area stores exceeded $400 million, and net earnings were $15 million, or $4.17 per share.

With all that success, it surprised me when Ed seemed so distracted at a New Year's Eve party at my home in Palm Beach in 1983. Toward the end of the evening, he mentioned that he had received a disturbing proposal from an aggressive and always ungracious New York investment advisor named Ronald S. Baron. Baron had called Hoffman to suggest a leveraged buyout of the company at a price 50 percent higher than the stock's current trading levels. Claiming to represent around 18 percent of the shareholders, Baron told Ed that he had already begun to line up bank support for a $300 million loan to complete the deal. Concerned that Baron's unsolicited activity would put the company in play, Ed asked if I would be interested in lending a hand if things got difficult. I assured him that I would do anything I could to help. The strength of Woodward & Lothrop was critical to the success of our Washington-area properties, which were performing very well. The last thing Woodies needed was an unwelcome distraction. Since the midseventies, Bloomingdale's, I. Magnin, and Neiman Marcus had come to town with strong competition for the hearts and wallets of the sophisticated D.C. shopper. Ed Hoffman knew he had to mind the store.

A few weeks later, Ron Baron called to invite me into his deal. I told him I wasn't interested. Around March 30, I got a call from Ed Hoffman asking if I would be interested in buying the company. The Woodies board was convinced they needed a white knight. The next day, a Saturday, Ed and his vice-chairman, Robert Mulligan, flew to Detroit to meet with me at my home in Bloomfield Hills. I made it clear that I would consider making an offer for the company only if Ed and his management team stayed on to run the business. If Ed was committed to Woodies, I was interested.

After about a month of due diligence, I made an offer through my investment bankers at Oppenheimer. Woodies was represented by Goldman Sachs. We arrived at a price of $59 per share, totaling $220 million, and negotiated an option—really an incentive to stay—for Ed, Bob Mulligan, and the company's talented president, David Mullen, to buy 20 percent of the company. The Woodward & Lothrop board of directors accepted the offer at their April 30 meeting.

The last step was for the shareholders to approve the deal. That didn't happen until late September. In the intervening months, Ron Baron and his investors sold their shares, but another interested buyer entered the picture. Monroe Milstein, owner of the Burlington Coat Factory Warehouse, made several attempts to raise the funds for a counteroffer. Given Milstein's reputation as a cost-cutting discounter, the merchants at Woodies were not thrilled with the prospect of his leadership. Burl Albright, a board member and former company executive, referred to the new suitor in the press as "an old cloakie," retailer shorthand for a coat buyer. Seeking the support of Woodward and Lothrop family members, Milstein kept just enough pressure on the board to delay the vote. Anxious to end the impasse, I upped my offer to $60.50 a share. That did it, and I became the proud new owner of Woodward & Lothrop, the largest retailer in the Washington market and the largest advertiser in the *Washington Post*. I flew home to Detroit, confident that I had a terrific management team in place to grow market share and protect the future value of the Taubman Company's Washington-area centers.

My confidence was misplaced.

One of the first signs of the trouble ahead came as Ed Hoffman and I were touring Nordstrom's flagship store in Seattle. I respected the chain's legendary reputation for customer service, and wanted Ed to see first-hand the level of competition we were facing with Nordstrom establishing a foothold in the Washington market. Halfway through our walk through the store, I realized that I had to make a phone call. Since we were in the dark, quiet days before cell phones, I asked a salesperson to direct me to the nearest pay phone. Instantly, she invited me behind the counter to use her department's phone. "You don't need to use a pay phone, sir. Just dial 9 and your number, and talk as long as you like."

We were witnessing the kind of inspired customer service Nordstrom was about to import to our backyard, the kind of service we weren't providing customers. Ed and I looked at each other and without words expressed the same thought: "We're screwed." As it turned out, we were indeed screwed. Our historic franchise was heading into a perfect storm. The stores, which had been neglected for many years, were in need of major, expensive renovation. The most urgent candidate for attention was the once-grand flagship store at the corner of 11th and G streets in downtown Washington, D.C. We spent the millions of dollars required to restore its luster, along with the funds needed to spruce up our suburban locations to compete with our competitors' newer stores. Nordstrom, Neiman Marcus, and Bloomingdale's were hurting us at the high end, and discounters entering the market were nipping at us at the other end.

Seeking to enhance our buying power, we formed national alliances and acquired the Philadelphia-based John Wanamaker chain in 1986. It, too, had an historic downtown flagship store in need of loving attention, which we provided, right down to the restoration of the nation's largest concert pipe organ.

We certainly kept our focus on improving the customer experience and enhancing our merchandise selection. Unfortunately, Ed Hoffman became less and less involved. Since I had purchased the company, Ed's golf handicap had improved by at least six strokes, and our best executive and merchant, David Mullen, had left for a job with the May Company. Running Woodies became an increasingly personal commitment on my part; a commitment for which I had little time or enthusiasm.

To be fair to Ed, the retailing industry was going through some dramatic change as we were struggling with Woodies' future. The Ed Hoffmans of the world had reached the top of their profession through taste and merchandising instinct—what we called "nose" in the industry. Increasingly, however, the department store game was one of numbers, computers, and sophisticated financing. I saw much the same disconnect from my vantage point as a board member and major investor at Macy's, where Ed Finkelstein—a great guy—had justly earned a reputation as a retailing genius. But as his attention turned from the latest fashions to leveraged buyouts and acquisitions, he proved to be a fish out of water. With debt tying the company's hands, several seasons of overbuying, and customers losing their enthusiasm for the stores, Macy's was ultimately acquired by Federated Stores in 1994—a company Macy's had often dreamed of owning. Ed played no role in the new conglomerate.

One holiday season, just a few days before Christmas, I received an impassioned phone call in my Detroit office from a customer in Washington. She had been shopping in Woodies' downtown flagship location and had been informed that the store had run out of Kringle Bears, a promotional item we were giving away with purchases over $100. An unthinking sales associate had commented to her that all the stuffed bears had been shipped to our suburban locations.

The customer was irate, and rightly so. "How dare you short-change us here in the city," she protested. "I'm going to call the *Washington Post.*" I hadn't heard such anger in a customer's voice since I made the decision to close all of the ice skating rinks we had in our malls (maintaining the ice was prohibitively expensive, and the attraction drew few new customers). Mothers called for weeks to let me know that I had single-handedly destroyed their daughters' chances of making the Olympic team!

It wasn't the threat to besmirch our character in the *Washington Post* that motivated me (the great Katharine Graham was a good friend, and we were, after all, the publication's largest advertiser). But I wanted to right this wrong. I took her number and quickly got to the bottom of the problem. Response to the promotion was so overwhelming, we were running out of Kringle Bears in every store. Nevertheless, I secured one of the few remaining bears and called the disappointed woman back. "This is Alfred Taubman, and I'm pleased to tell you that we have a Kringle Bear waiting for you at the downtown store. Or if you like, we will deliver it to your home."

There was silence for several seconds, and then she spoke in a slow, deep voice: "Sir, do you know what the weather is like here in Washington right now?"

"No, I'm in Detroit today."

"Well, it's around twenty degrees and snowing."

"Then please, let us deliver the bear to you."

Again there was silence. And then she let me have it. "Now I *am* calling the *Post*. What kind of man would take a young bear out in such weather? The poor thing will surely catch a cold. Now, listen here: you hold that bear for me at the store until it warms up enough to safely transport him home. And for God's sake, keep him warm until I come or I will call the *Post!*"

I didn't feel much like a white knight anymore. And the feeling just got worse as it became clear that even with new management—in 1989 Ed Hoffman retired and was replaced by former Saks executive Arnold Aronson—there was no future for this venerable department store chain. We had become a dinosaur. We had lost our relevance to the customer and lacked the agility to change course. Despite being encouraged by my bankers and financial advisers to place Woodies into bankruptcy, I delayed that decision for a year to see if we could turn things around. I owed that to our 12,000 employees and their families. In the end, we couldn't make it work. But we did succeed—at significant personal cost to me—in transferring ownership of every store location to other retail chains in the market. Not a single store-level job was lost.

Did the Woodies experience kill my enthusiasm for the department store? No. As with everything, there are good department stores and department stores that don't deserve to survive. Well-run, properly financed companies will continue to thrive. And while extraordinary consolidation continues to take place in the industry, the organizations still standing are well positioned for growth and profitability. The customers in Taubman centers respond very positively to the merchandise and service provided by such powerful brands as Saks Fifth Avenue, Nordstrom, Neiman Marcus, Bloomingdale's, Macy's, Dillard's, and JCPenney. These retailers stand for something special, they stand out with promotional punch, and they consistently nurture customer confidence.

The most successful malls will continue to be anchored by these powerful people pumps. And creative developers will continue to combine a host of different major offerings to deliver traffic to their specialty store tenants. In several Taubman malls, for instance, the total sales of the center's restaurants equal the revenue of a traditional anchor. Large home furnishings and design centers are certainly good candidates for anchor locations in certain markets. Remember, in the days of the urban arcade, train stations and cathedrals functioned as very effective anchors for major retail destinations.

But the Woodies experience teaches a critical lesson for any entrepreneur considering an acquisition of any size: People run businesses. Great people run great businesses. Stanley Marcus ran a magnificent store. My good friend Marvin Traub made Bloomingdale's "like no other store in the world." But Ed Hoffman lost his passion for Woodies, and Arnold Aronson never moved from New York to Washington to really get his nose into the business.

So if you are not absolutely sure that a great management team is in place or can be recruited quickly, don't buy the business unless you intend to run it yourself. And if you see yourself in that role, be sure you have the time to devote as much attention as you focused on your original business when it was first getting off the ground.

It's all about minding the store.

– NINE –

Fashion Statement

In the current retail climate, it's difficult for department stores and other large retailers to compete if they stake out the middle ground. One of the defining features of our economy in the past few decades has been the growth and expansion of luxury retailers. And for almost as long as we've been in business, we've focused on appealing to the luxury retailing customer. Again, this involved overcoming threshold resistance. Because while comparatively few people can afford to do all their shopping at high-end stores like Tiffany's or Neiman Marcus, a lot of people can afford to do *some* of their shopping at such stores. That's why the world of fashion has expanded so rapidly.

In the shopping center business, we classify certain anchor tenants as "fashion" department stores. For example, Neiman Marcus and Saks Fifth Avenue are fashion department stores. Sears and JCPenney, better known for housewares and hard goods, are not. Nor are Marshall Field's or Macy's, which are classified as "full-line" department stores. They sell all categories of department store-type merchandise, shorthanded in the retailing business as DSTM. Yes, they carry some moderate-to-medium fashion apparel, but a true fashion department store's merchandise mix focuses on medium-to-better goods and essentially no hard lines.

Mass merchandisers Wal-Mart or Kmart are not even close to being fashion contenders. Target wants very badly to be perceived as a fashion merchant, and is having some success (thanks in large measure to terrific advertising). Of course, these stores sell apparel, but customers look only to certain retailers for true fashion.

The term *fashion* is used loosely and is rarely well-defined. But the concept makes a big difference to the consumer and the merchant. The popularity, pricing, and promotion of fashion items can be very different from merchandise lacking this imprimatur. In essence, the fundamental quality that elevates anything into the fashion category is *design*. Not just any design: good design that appeals to your taste. Fashion is added-value through design. And we're not just talking about apparel.

For most of world history, fashion was the exclusive domain of the very rich. Style was driven by the royal families of Europe, and only the highest levels of landed gentry could hope to mimic their taste. This began to change in the late nineteenth and early twentieth centuries along with mass merchandising and the growth of the middle class in the United States and Europe. The shopping mall (Taubman properties included) helped strengthen this revolution in commerce. Marvin Traub in his terrific autobiography, *Like No Other Store . . . : The Bloomingdale's Legend and the Revolution in American Marketing*, focuses on this historic transition:

> In the 1930s and 1940s, as I was growing up, shopping was, for most people, a basic function . . . before the Second World War, most department stores offered goods the way Henry Ford sold the Model T—you could have any color as long as it was black. Lipstick came in very few shades, and appliances and garden supplies were sold alongside cameras, radios, and religious items.
>
> My parents were friends with some of the most glamorous retailers and celebrities of their time; through them, I saw a cachet and

style that was available only to a small circle of sophisticated shoppers, people who shopped at Bonwit Teller, Bergdorf Goodman, Saks Fifth Avenue, and Neiman Marcus. A generation later, Bloomingdale's brought that cachet and sense of fashion authority to a larger audience, a new kind of shopper created by the growing wealth of post–World War II America. To the basic concepts of good taste and good value, Bloomingdale's added entertainment and style.

In recent decades, the fashion and design revolution has expanded into realms far beyond apparel. As consumer choice expanded, and as retailers and manufacturers aimed to build and serve new tastes and markets, design became an important consideration, not just for the growing of mass luxury products, but for all products.

Consider a wastebasket, an everyday item you can purchase in any number of retail venues. You're looking for a certain size or shape, or perhaps you want it to be waterproof, and you might want it to have a lid. For a few bucks, you can buy a terrific plastic wastebasket (in an array of colors) at Wal-Mart to satisfy all these functional criteria. For a few extra dollars, it can even be a brand-name wastebasket, like Rubbermaid, sure to last for years without any trouble.

But for most consumers, utility is not the only consideration—even when buying a wastebasket. In a den, library, or bedroom, plastic will not do. The choices now extend to wicker, brass, leather, wood. Given the decor in the room, maybe a hand-painted wastebasket purchased during a vacation at the seashore would be perfect. Such a wastebasket will command a higher price than the Rubbermaid alternative. You have a story to tell your friends about the purchase, and you expect something so different, perhaps even unique, to cost more. The wonderful world beyond utility is the world of fashion. Here, design makes the difference, and the customer will pay for this added value. In fact, the closer an item comes to actually being unique, the more a merchant can justify a higher price tag (again, if the design is good).

When Karl Lagerfeld designs a one-of-a-kind evening gown for an individual customer, that's fashion at the highest level. The Lagerfeld couture dress wears and presses better than a more utilitarian garment. It is made to fit a particular person's proportions perfectly, and flatters her hair color as well as her station in life. That's the promise of couture. In a world of standardization and mass production, it makes what you might call a very personal fashion statement.

But one of the defining characteristics of our retailing age has been the democratization of fashion, the offering and creation of luxury products for a broad audience. After all, retailers at all price points are always striving for ways to differentiate themselves and offer customers something special. When Karl Lagerfeld designs for a popular merchant like H&M (a Swedish retailer known for very inexpensive but fashionable young people's apparel), a significant amount of fashion magic still comes through to the consumer. The H&M shopper feels great about herself, even if the blouse may fall apart after just a few washings.

Fashion can even be found in the kitchen or bathrooms of American homes. Chances are, you and your spouse have puzzled over just the right choice of faucets, dishware, towels, and pots and pans. Stores like Williams-Sonoma, Crate and Barrel, Pottery Barn, and Pier 1 Imports have created excitement around everyday utensils and products you may not have equated with fashion. Architect Michael Graves's iconic teakettle, designed exclusively for Target customers, is a perfect example of successful fashion merchandising at a moderate price point (more expensive than a standard-issue teakettle, but inexpensive nonetheless). Martha Stewart's sheets, towels, and pots and pans at Kmart are also examples of added-value through design. Customers feel confident in Martha's taste (as well as her commitment to quality) and will pay a bit more to bring her products into their homes. They feel better about the purchase. And it is no coincidence that as a general rule, Martha's merchandise is by far the most successful of any offered by Kmart.

These trends have propelled the growth of our company. Most of our centers are located today in upscale areas, and are full of retailers who are engaged in selling luxury design and fashion products to a much larger customer base than they could have imagined.

But while consumers plainly see the value of the distinctive offerings, stock analysts don't. Now, so you don't think I'm always this rude, I should explain that one question stock analysts always ask me is, "How long will it take, Mr. Taubman, for Wal-Mart to kill every department store and fashion mall in the country?"

Before answering, I always turn the tables. I ask: "How many of you, men and women, are wearing an item of clothing purchased at Wal-Mart, raise your hands?" Over the last twenty years I must have asked my Wal-Mart question more than a hundred times to untold numbers of confident, well-dressed analysts. No one has ever raised a hand.

Then I ask my second question: "Raise your hand if a friend or anyone in your family has ever purchased an item of apparel at Wal-Mart?" Again, zero. Twenty years, not a single hand.

Hands down, Wal-Mart is the most powerful retailer in the world and the largest company of any kind on the planet. So why aren't they in the fashion and design business? Sure, the company has made deals with designers to create product lines that are sold exclusively at Wal-Mart. But that has not drawn shoppers. Beyond good design, there are other, more intangible aspects of fashion merchandising we can't overlook. As Marvin Traub pointed out, taste and image have a lot to do with it. Most consumers appreciate and trust the taste level of Michael Graves, Martha Stewart, and Karl Lagerfeld. Millions of dollars and years of proven success have defined such fashion brands as Polo, Coach, Louis Vuitton, and Gucci in the minds and hearts of shoppers around the world. That didn't happen overnight.

Wal-Mart is also a powerful brand. It stands for many important promises, most having to do with price—an attribute less critical to fashion. The down-home, mass-merchandiser, low-price-every-day image that makes Wal-Mart so successful at what it does runs counter to what shoppers expect from Neiman Marcus or Saks. Can you picture the typical senior citizen Wal-Mart greeter standing at the entrance to a Polo store asking if you've seen the latest newspaper sale circular? To a fashion-conscious shopper, that presents serious threshold resistance.

Stock analysts aren't the only ones who overestimate Wal-Mart's ability to eat into the business of department stores and specialty retailers. Several years ago I participated in a real estate industry panel with Sam Zell, a successful commercial real estate developer (and a fellow University of Michigan Wolverine). "There is no place left for the department store," Sam confidently proclaimed, before going on to predict the absolute retail dominance of Wal-Mart in the United States. Now, Sam knows a lot more about office buildings than he does about retail properties. And the fundamentals of the two businesses are very different, as are the roles of the developer.

Major mall development is an *operating* business. The economics are based on a business opportunity—the ability of a merchant to produce sales volume by serving a specific market. The developer provides the environment—physical, locational, promotional, operational—to optimize the merchant's performance. It's a long-term commitment that, if all goes well, yields long-term rewards and continues to add value for both merchant and developer.

Office buildings, by contrast, are a *commodities* business. Price is usually more important in determining the success of a property than other factors such as location, design, and access. In fact, prestige, ego, civic responsibilities, or even personal quirks may drive the development decision. I once asked an executive with a national retailer why his company had chosen an out-of-the-way site for a new headquarters building. He explained that the CEO had rejected multiple locations recommended by his real estate and marketing departments in favor of a site five miles from his home and ten minutes from his country club.

If you are an employee in a major corporation, chances are you will show up for work at the office Monday morning despite the highway gridlock, lousy parking, and uninspiring views. Try adding those inconveniences and turnoffs to a retail location, and you're looking at bankruptcy. They're fundamentally different businesses, and that's why most successful developers stick to one or the other.

In the 1980s, the Taubman Company became involved with some mixed-use projects. In Charleston we created Charleston Place, a hotel, conference, and shopping complex in the heart of one of America's most historic downtowns. And in Manhattan, we were partners with Solomon Equities in 712 Fifth Avenue, a Kohn Pedersen Fox—designed fifty-two-story luxury office tower in the heart of Midtown at 56th Street. At the base of the building, which opened in 1990, are three historic Fifth Avenue townhouses, which we preserved (with the help of the architectural restoration firm Beyer Blinder Belle) to the delight of the city's very demanding Municipal Arts Society (once headed by Jacqueline Kennedy Onassis). We renovated these structures, which were once home to such legendary retailers as Cartier and the Rizzoli bookstore, and leased them to my friend Les Wexner, who had just purchased Henri Bendel.

There are real estate developers who excel in multiple property formats. Donald Trump is one of the very few high-profile practitioners with success in the commercial, retail, residential, and recreational segments of our business. He's intelligent (he got a lot of his real estate smarts from his father, Fred, whom I knew pretty well) and has branded himself in a unique way. The Trump name adds interest, excitement, and most important of all, value. Donald's golf course properties are planned and executed beautifully, as are his office towers and luxury residential projects. And he's a television star!

Sam Zell, who has enjoyed great success with office buildings, is not so multitalented. So when he made his uninformed pronouncement, I had to challenge his retail expertise. I looked at his shirt and asked my favorite question: "Sam, did you buy that shirt you're wearing at Wal-Mart?" Sam's shirt could have been purchased at Wal-Mart. I know double-needle stitching when I see it. Rather than raise his hand or counter my point, Sam simply glared at me for the rest of the session. I think if we weren't both Wolverines—and I weren't about a foot taller and a hundred pounds heavier than he is—he would have hit me.

Now, it's possible that Sam and other high-powered, well-paid Wall Street types just don't want us to know they shop at Wal-Mart, or are hesitant to admit that they know people who do. I would argue that such a defensive response is just as negative for any retailer hoping to be known for fashion merchandise. Embarrassment is not an enviable brand promise! Don't get me wrong—Wal-Mart has and will continue to kill certain retailers and certain malls, legitimately so. Malls featuring a mix of me-too stores carrying generic, lower-priced merchandise are directly in Wal-Mart's crosshairs.

That's one important reason why Taubman malls have always been focused on luxury and fashion merchandise. For any retail enterprise, the farther away from Wal-Mart you are, the better! And you can't get any further away than the world of fashion.

So what about off-price outlets that carry designer goods for less? Don't they offer all the magic of fashion merchandise at much lower prices? If Wal-Mart isn't going to put the higher-end malls and department stores out of business, won't the discount malls at least do some damage?

It's time for another universal truth: *There can be no off-price without full price.* In other words, what makes the purchase of a 100 percent cotton Polo tennis shirt for $30 so special is the fact that somewhere else a Polo tennis shirt is selling for $75. Close Polo's mall shops and take Polo products out of the men's department at Neiman Marcus, and you destroy the entire enterprise, including the appeal of the off-price outlets.

A quick story to illustrate this very important point.

Years ago, there was a successful line of affordable silverware marketed as Wm. Rogers silver. The company's silver-plated flatware, which came in a broad selection of styles, from colonial to contemporary, was sold exclusively in jewelry stores. Young couples would sit across from the jewelers, learning about the various designs and determining the right pattern for their lifestyles. Like most consumers, the young couples lacked confidence in their ability to make such important purchase decisions without assistance from a knowledgeable salesperson. The jeweler conveniently played that role (chances are, the couple was buying their wedding rings and registering many of the wedding gifts they wanted at this same jeweler).

In the late 1960s, management decided to strengthen sales by also offering their product through the E. J. Korvette discount chain. Customers could purchase the flatware for almost 30 percent less than they would have to pay in their local jewelry store. At first, Wm. Rogers silverware flew off the shelves. The company was pleased with this new mass distribution channel.

Of course, the jewelers were not so pleased. Increasingly, young couples would come into the jewelers for the helpful tutorial, then go across town to Korvette's and purchase at discount the pattern they decided on with the patient jeweler's assistance. Within months, jewelers stopped devoting any counter space or sales time to Wm. Rogers. Couples could try to get some help from the clueless Korvette's sales people (if they could get their attention at all), but in the truest sense, they were on their own. Samples of the various patterns were routinely stolen off cheap-looking display boards.

Within a very short time, Wm. Rogers ceased to exist. The company learned the hard way that there can be no off-price without full-price. Once the jewelers abandoned the product, Wm. Rogers silver became just another discount brand, not the special heirloom purchase newlyweds felt confident about making.

So how does a retailer maintain a sustainable balance between its full-price and off-price merchandise? In the days of the dominant, massive downtown department stores, the answer was as close as the basement. These merchants had enough room right in their stores to offer last season's and other stale merchandise on the lower level of the building. This outlet level allowed the department store to clear out the upper floors for new merchandise, while controlling the presentation of their marked-down items. The lower-level display space was far less opulent, and there were fewer salespeople on hand to assist. But shoppers could be confident that the store stood behind every purchase, and manufacturers could be confident that the store was still presenting their brands appropriately.

As department store companies built smaller, basement-less suburban branch stores, there was no space for these outlet operations. Recognizing an outstanding opportunity, chain discounters like Marshalls and T. J. Maxx took over the distribution of this off-price merchandise, paying the department stores cents on the dollar. Manufacturers, as you might guess, were far less comfortable with this arrangement. The further away from their control the merchandise got, and the deeper the discounts became, the more difficult it was to maintain a strong brand image. The delicate balance between full price and off-price was spinning out of control.

That's when manufacturers and department stores decided to open their own branded off-price outlet stores. Outlet malls sprang up in the 1980s and 1990s, usually comfortable distances from traditional mall properties, featuring such attractive outlets as Saks's Off 5th, Neiman Marcus's Last Call Clearance Center, Nordstrom Rack, and numerous manufacturer stores. The retailers felt good about these new locations, just as they felt good decades earlier about the off-price operations in their basements.

But the challenge remains: The delicate balance between full price and off-price must be maintained. Knowing just when the balance goes out of kilter is more art than science. But as many retailers have found out, paying attention to the recipe is critical to the survival of even the strongest brands. This reality may be the single most important governor of the future growth of Costco and Sam's Club.

– TEN –

Sold!

Throughout the early years of my career, as I made enough money to look beyond the basic needs of my family, my passion for art grew into a pretty substantial art collection. In the 1950s, I was a regular visitor to the Green Galleries on West 57th Street in New York, where a rickety elevator took you to the fourth floor. There, dealer Richard Bellamy proudly introduced you to fresh works by the likes of Robert Indiana, Jasper Johns, and Francis Bacon. I started buying modern artists like Frank Stella and Robert Rauschenberg. Later, I bought from Leo Castelli.

Much of what I collected I purchased on credit, and I studied hard enough to develop a good eye for quality. As my business became more successful, I became a regular customer of art dealers and auction houses around the world. At the same time, I was honored to serve on the boards of the Whitney Museum of American Art in New York, the Smithsonian Institution's Archives of American Art, and the Detroit Institute of Arts, where I have proudly fulfilled the responsibilities of arts commissioner of the city of Detroit (the closest I ever want to come to elected office, for more than twenty years).

So I was not entirely in the dark when I received an interesting phone call in the spring of 1983—just weeks after I completed the sale of my stake in the Irvine Ranch—from David Westmorland, former chairman of Sotheby's, international auction house. The Earl of Westmorland explained he had heard from a mutual friend, David Metcalfe, that I might be interested in promising investment opportunities. He asked if I would be available to meet with him regarding Sotheby's, and offered to come to Detroit at my earliest convenience.

Of course, David Metcalfe had already introduced me to another wonderful opportunity in my life. About a year earlier, David, who provided insurance services to the Taubman Company, called me to arrange an interview for a young woman named Judith Rounick. I had seen Judy at a few dinner parties but had never had the chance to speak with her at any length. All I knew was that she always was the most beautiful woman in the room.

We met for lunch at La Côte Basque in New York for what was intended to be a discussion of her career direction (Judy was in the middle of a divorce and wanted to pursue new interests). She was very intelligent and all business. I was mesmerized. She had grown up in Israel, spoke several languages, and was the mother of two children. She carried herself with extraordinary grace and, of course, was the most beautiful woman in the room. I'm sure my advice, like my concentration, was worthless that day. All I could think about through lunch was the next time I could see her.

At the time I had been divorced for five years. Reva and I had grown apart, mostly because I had buried myself in my business and spent far too much time away from home. Reva was a terrific mother, and I had been a far better father than husband. Sure, I missed more than my share of parent-teacher conferences, student plays, and football games, but I included my children in my life whenever I had the chance. My son Bobby fondly remembers "taking picnics on construction sites," and Billy remembers "attacking" my briefcase whenever I came home. And I'm confident my daughter, Gayle, developed her love of art during our many visits to museums around the world.

Whenever I'm asked to identify my greatest accomplishment, it's always the same answer: my children.

In 1977, with little animosity, Reva and I decided to go our own ways after twenty-nine years of marriage. At the final divorce meeting with our respective attorneys, I turned over documents declaring my net worth. It was a pretty substantial number. Reva's reaction confirmed for me that we were making the right decision. Examining the papers, she turned to her counsel and said, "He's always showing off. He's not worth anywhere near that amount." Reva was not a negotiator.

After five years as a bachelor, I was convinced that I would never marry again. And then everything changed at La Côte Basque. Judy and I dated for a couple of months, but I could never convince her to visit me at my home in Palm Beach. I think she thought that was too much of a commitment so soon in our relationship. She even turned me down when I invited her to attend a small dinner party for Henry Ford II at Estée Lauder's Palm Beach home. After I called Estée (one of the most successful, talented women in the world) to explain that I would be coming alone, she immediately asked for Judy's phone number. I figured that it wouldn't hurt to get a character reference from Estée Lauder. And it worked. Judy agreed to accompany me to the party. After that weekend, I was determined to keep her in my life. We were married four months later.

So when Lord Westmorland called with the Sotheby's opportunity at the recommendation of David Metcalfe, I agreed to meet. I can't say that I was immediately enthusiastic. Sotheby's was surely a venerable company and an outstanding brand. Samuel Baker, the uncle of John Sotheby, held his first auction of books in London in 1744, which makes Sotheby's older than the United States of America, not to mention older than its archrival, Christie's.

Despite its dominant position as one of only two truly international art auction houses, Sotheby's had been regularly operating in the red and was embroiled in a contentious takeover battle with American investors Marshall Cogan and Stephen Swid. (The company had gone public in 1977.) Sotheby's insiders—publicly expressing outrage with more than a touch of anti-Semitism—had taken to calling the unfriendly raiders "Toboggan and Skid." One of the company's senior experts promised to resign if a sale to the Americans were consummated; another threatened to commit suicide. How would these Brits feel about a Jewish shopping center developer from Detroit?

The meeting at my home in Bloomfield Hills with the very distinguished Lord Westmorland went well. The board was not pleased with Cogan and Swid and did not agree with their vision for the company. Business reforms and cost reductions put in place by Sotheby's new chairman, Gordon Brunton—an executive on loan from the successful Thomson publishing empire—were showing results. And the company was looking for a white knight (the same role I would be thrust into with Woodies).

Throughout my life I had thought of myself in all sorts of roles: father, husband, businessman, soldier, developer, golfer (well, sort of), even art collector. But a white knight? I didn't own a set of armor and was not great on horseback. And I kept reminding myself that for every fair maiden a white knight encountered, there were dragons, sorcerers, and legions of warriors wanting his head!

Next, Peter Wilson, who had led Sotheby's through its most successful years of growth and profitability, visited with me in my New York apartment. He was a tall, inspiring character and an amazing salesman. I remember his magnificent voice and the sincere passion he expressed for the business. I promised to take a hard look at the company.

The harder I looked, the more I liked the opportunity. At the time, there was an annual turnover of fine art around the world of approximately $25 billion. Yet with all that art changing hands every year, Sotheby's and Christie's together accounted for less than $1 billion in sales. That left a tremendous share of the art market up for grabs. Sotheby's had a unique franchise, a strong worldwide reputation for expertise, and there were enormous barriers to entry in the art auction business. You couldn't just print a catalog, rent a hall, and hold an auction in this rarified world of art, authenticity, and prestige. As a customer, I thought I knew just where improvements could be made to build on the company's assets. Sotheby's wasn't a retail business like the retailers I had come to know as a landlord and investor—and therein lay an opportunity.

Like all other auction houses, Sotheby's had always catered primarily to dealers, or as they say, the trade. Professional art dealers would purchase items at auction for essentially wholesale prices and mark them up substantially for retail sale in their shops. Only a relatively small number of individuals—usually very wealthy individuals—had the confidence to buy directly at auction. Those who did, found the experience to be fun and rewarding.

I was one of those individuals, and I was convinced that a much broader market of potential auction customers existed in the United States and around the world. Every day, at our centers, I saw the growing interest among a broad swathe of consumers in design, in fashion, in mass luxury. Now, Sotheby's could never attract the volume of traffic that thronged to Woodfield every day. But there was more to the auction house than million-dollar impressionist and old master paintings. People buying wall-to-wall carpeting for their living rooms could instead bid on unique 150-year-old Persian carpets. Unlike factory-made carpets, these beautiful heirlooms would continue to gain in value over the years and stimulate conversation at every dinner party. People wanting to enliven their homes with antiques could meet with Sotheby's experts to experience the joys of collecting. People seeking enriching entertainment could attend Sotheby's exhibitions and participate in exciting, glamorous auctions in energy-filled auction rooms.

As I saw it, Sotheby's also had some distinct advantages over re-tailers. The items (or lots) auctioned at Sotheby's were sold on con-signment, which meant the business operated without the normal, and very real, inventory risks experienced by traditional retailers. Unlike Macy's or Woodward & Lothrop, Sotheby's did not have to lay out significant capital for inventory and hope that things would sell. The auction house was simply creating a marketplace for the ex-change of other people's property.

I really shouldn't use the word "simply." Creating a vibrant, ra-tional worldwide marketplace for art is anything but simple. Sotheby's had been working at it for more than two centuries. But there was a powerful force keeping individuals out of the auction rooms and holding Sotheby's back from dramatically increasing its business and market share: threshold resistance.

I had experienced it myself at both Sotheby's and Christie's. Even though I was a good customer, an avid collector, and financially well-off, representatives at both houses were rude, unresponsive, and often condescending. Had they been shoe salesmen, they wouldn't have lasted long in any store in any Taubman mall. God help you if you had the nerve to visit an auction house expert seek-ing an opinion about Grandma's silver or Uncle Frank's sporting pic-ture. It's hard to overstate the level of consumer angst created by these institutions. Buying art at auction was perceived as a rich person's sport. Unless you were a dealer or a duke, stepping over the threshold of a major auction house took real courage and self-confidence. An appointment at the dentist was far more appealing. At least the dentist doesn't question your taste and insult your possessions.

"Christie's are gentlemen trying to be businessmen, and Sotheby's are businessmen trying to be gentlemen," a popular line went. But I couldn't find much evidence that either house was particularly gen-tlemanly or businesslike. And the auction process itself, for most people, was drenched in threshold resistance. What if I sneeze? Will I own the Van Gogh? Didn't that happen to Lucy and Ethel on an episode of *I Love Lucy*? And what should my strategy be in the salesroom? Should I bid early, or wait for the last possible moment to raise my paddle for the first time?

I believed that if we could break down the threshold resistance, the auction business could be transformed into a far broader, more profitable enterprise. And this could be accomplished without jeopardizing any of the glitz, glamour, or prestige of the business or the company. But would the leadership of Sotheby's trust me to make some fundamental changes to their attitude and business without taking their own lives?

For whatever reason, I was immediately more palatable than "Toboggan and Skid." Having earned a name for themselves by acquiring and repositioning undervalued companies, Cogan and Swid were proud owners of General Felt Industries and Knoll Group, a respected manufacturer of modern furniture. Cogan was on the board of the Museum of Modern Art. Lord Westmorland informed me, however, that Sotheby's first face-to-face meeting with the American entrepreneurs had been a disaster. He assured me, however, that the boys on New Bond Street (where the company had been headquartered since 1917) were looking forward to meeting me.

It turned out to be one of the strangest encounters of my life. My attorney and trusted adviser, Jeffrey Miro, and I were invited to dinner in London with a dozen or so Sotheby's directors, officers, and experts. Physically, Jeffrey and I could be described as an odd couple. I am six feet two inches tall and have been described by the never very sensitive press as "burly," "portly," and "bear-like." Jeffrey, on the other hand, is about five-six and boyishly thin. I wear three-piece suits; he prefers blazers and bow ties.

We all gathered in the jewelry department, across the street from Sotheby's London headquarters. There was a large rectangular table in the wood-paneled room. As we took our assigned seats, Gordon

Brunton announced that Jeffrey and I would stay put at our places across from each other throughout the meal, but that every fifteen minutes, when a bell rang, Sotheby's personnel would shift one seat to their left with their plates, glasses, and utensils. This unusual version of musical chairs was designed to create the opportunity for each executive to chat directly with "the Americans" during dinner.

Chat we did, for several hours. It actually turned out to be informative and fun. As my wife, Judy, will tell you, I always eat too fast and enjoy talking through dinner. Jeffrey and I would exchange reassuring glances with each rotation, taking advantage of the momentary lull to swallow some food. We learned a lot about Sotheby's with each new conversation, and they learned as much or more about us. Other than trying to get a better idea of my taste and knowledge of art, their top concern was stability—would I commit to stick around and provide the financial strength to operate in something other than crisis mode. (They grilled Jeffrey, too, who held his own just fine. His wife, Marsha, was the arts editor at the *Detroit Free Press,* and Jeffrey has an extraordinary business mind.)

In a very real sense, with every personal exchange we were overcoming threshold resistance—their resistance to us. Throughout life, everyone faces similar challenges. Maybe it's an acquaintance you would like to know better, a banker you want to impress, or an investor you'd like to buy shares in your company. In each of these scenarios, the most important things are to listen and be yourself. Because Jeffrey and I were just as interested in the quality and concerns of Sotheby's management as they were in our vision for their business, we listened carefully to their concerns and ideas. We also didn't pretend to be auctioneers or authorities on Chinese porcelain. We were businessmen, marketers, and lovers of art.

Despite its unorthodox choreography, the dinner was a success. You could sense that these executives loved what they did and had the greatest respect for their company. We seemed to have a

common view of the business and where it could go. Encouraged by
Brunton and Westmorland to make an offer, I bought out the interests of Cogan and Swid and assembled an investor group. Joining me
were several of my Irvine Ranch partners: Max Fisher, Henry Ford II,
and Milton Petrie, along with Les Wexner, Connecticut residential
real estate executive Bill Pitt, art publisher Alexis Gregory, Italian
businessman Emilio Gioia, and Ambassador Earl E. T. Smith, the former mayor of Palm Beach who had served as our nation's last, pre-
Castro ambassador to Cuba. Each of my friends brought valuable
perspective and relationships to the table. I put up $38.5 million for
60 percent of the stock, while my fellow investors contributed around
$30 million, and we borrowed $70 million from Chase Manhattan
Bank. Members of the art press, especially Rita Reif of the *New York
Times,* were apoplectic over the $139 million purchase price, which
they considered far too high. Their analysis of the deal reminded me
of the early reviews of my Irvine Ranch acquisition. For the record, as
I write this book (October 2006), I sold a portion of my Sotheby's
stock in 1992 for about $100 million, received dividends over the years
the company has been public of $100 million, received $168 million
in September 2005 for half my remaining stock, in April 2006 sold
3.98 million shares for $110 million, and still own a 4.9 percent stake
valued at more than $100 million (based on the company's share
price as of January 16, 2007). Even when you factor in inflation, that's
not a bad performance for an initial investment of $38.5 million. I re-
spect Rita and her art journalist colleagues very much, but rarely
consult with them for stock tips.

Our offer was enough to close the deal with Sotheby's public
shareholders and place the matter before the UK's Monopolies and
Mergers Commission, which must approve any investment in a public company by a foreign investor of more than a certain percent.

The situation was complicated by the fact that Sotheby's wasn't
just another British company. It was considered a British national

treasure. For centuries it had honorably administered the transfer of precious property—first books and then the entire spectrum of fine and decorative art—from one generation to another. The distinguished members of the Monopolies and Mergers Commission wanted to make sure that an American owner would respect the institution's traditions and assure the company's survival.

My hearing before this august body should have been intimidating, but I actually enjoyed answering the commissioners' questions. I also apparently raised some eyebrows when I personally greeted each member after they took their seats in the chamber, introducing myself with a handshake over the dais. Apparently, that had never been done before. But we got along famously. The transaction was blessed and completed in September 1983.

Sotheby's was now a privately owned company incorporated in Michigan with dual headquarters in London and New York. Just a few days after taking control, I turned my attention to the firm's most important asset—its people. It was time for some straight talk and tough love. I had the deepest respect for the expertise and talent of our associates, but I was far less satisfied with the level of service we provided to our clients at every level. "Being knowledgeable," I explained, "does not give us the right to be rude."

From now on, Sotheby's was going to embrace a service mentality and treat everyone with respect. We were going to introduce the auction experience to a broader audience of consumers around the world and encourage the development of new collectors and connoisseurs. Together we were going to open up and make more transparent what had been traditionally a closed and unnecessarily intimidating business.

In short, we were going to break down the threshold resistance that had been holding us back and stifling the art market for as long as I could remember.

To deliver this frank but energizing message face-to-face, I started the day with an all-staff meeting in London, jumped on the Concorde, flew into Kennedy International Airport, and addressed the troops in New York as they arrived for work. The Concorde, rest its soul, made the trans-Atlantic trip in three and a half hours. So with the five-hour time difference and the absence of e-mail, I was able to limit the preemption of my message between offices.

In both London and New York I could sense sincere enthusiasm and a great deal of relief. It's stressful to come to work wondering if your company and job will survive the day. It's equally frustrating to see little growth or improvement in your industry. That's what it had been like for the employees of Sotheby's. If nothing else, I offered resources, stability, and a much clearer vision of where we wanted to go. Even though change was a significant part of my message, the vast majority of my new colleagues in London and New York welcomed the challenge and expressed their support.

Over the next few years we had great fun breaking down barriers, winning new customers, and selling some of the most interesting art, antiques, and collectibles ever offered at auction.

We also made a few enemies.

– ELEVEN –

Cookie Jars and Irises

Management consultants and business school professors have developed all sorts of methods and approaches to positioning or repositioning a company for growth. The *Harvard Business Review* introduces new acronyms and fancy names with every issue. Developing things like missions, visions, and values is certainly helpful in getting everybody on the same page. But there is one other thing I like to do to stimulate management's creative juices.

Identify the forces and factors keeping your customers from coming over your threshold. Be honest. Brutally honest. If you're operating a restaurant, consider the quality of the food as well as its price and presentation. Does your menu appeal to your clientele? Analyze the comfort and character of your premises. Does the music playing in the background set the proper mood? Is your location convenient for your target customers? What about your waitstaff? Are they dressed appropriately, and focused on service and responsiveness? What restaurant options are in your immediate trade area, and what makes them popular?

If you're a trustee of a private high school struggling with declining enrollment, be honest, brutally honest. Is the faculty top-notch; are the facilities competitive? Are your graduates getting into the colleges they and their parents respect most? Do you offer the right sports and extracurricular activities? Is your reputation what it should be? Are there any major problems with the student body—drugs, discipline, attitude?

Analyzing threshold resistance is difficult because it's always easier to talk with the existing customers, the ones who have already crossed over your threshold. Of course, their opinions are critically important, and you don't want to lose their business or weaken their loyalty. But to grow, you have to bring new people into the store. Most companies—especially new businesses—don't have the money to bring in Yankelovich as we did at A&W. But even firms with very small budgets can take the crucial first step of being brutally honest with themselves. Challenge your management team with this assignment: "Let's pretend that we leave our company and create the toughest competitor we've ever faced. What would we do to beat us? How would we do things differently and better? What would we keep the same? Remember; we want to win, and the opponent is us!"

Shortly after we took Sotheby's private and I had recruited a new chief executive officer, I posed similar questions to the auction house's senior managers. "Let's walk across the street and start a new art auction company to beat our brains in," I said. "Don't hang on to the things we've been doing for two hundred years unless they're worth saving. You know our weaknesses, you know our strengths. You know the improvements you've always wanted to implement but were told you couldn't. Now's your chance. Sotheby's is the best auction company in the world, but we can beat us!"

We had a creative team in place, and this fun but very serious exercise got their creative juices flowing.

Michael Ainslie, our new CEO, stepped right out of central casting. Just forty-one years old, the tall, preppy southern gentleman exuded confidence and trust. Educated at Vanderbilt and Harvard, he had joined us from his role as president of the National Trust for Historic Preservation in Washington, D.C.

John Marion, our vice-chairman, was a legend in the auction world. His skills as an auctioneer and salesman were exceeded only by his Irish wit and charm. John, whose father was Louis Marion, an early partner and later the president of Parke-Bernet, an auction house in New York (which Sotheby's purchased in 1964 to establish a presence in the U.S.), had literally grown up in the business and had commanded the gavel at some of the most high-profile auctions in history. It was not unusual for customers to consign their property to Sotheby's with the condition that John be the auctioneer on the evening their treasure was offered for sale.

Diana "Dede" Brooks, who had joined the company several years earlier essentially as a volunteer, was a decisive, fast-rising financial executive. She had been a member of the first female graduating class at Yale, and her background as a senior loan officer at Citibank made her stand out from the typical Sotheby's associate. Frankly, so did her energy, self-assurance, and aggressiveness (traits that would later metastasize into recklessness and dishonesty).

James Lally, an accomplished Chinese porcelain expert with an MBA, was the president of our North American operations. Jim, who today runs his own very successful art dealership, never appeared comfortable in our early strategy meetings. I'm not sure he bought into my exercise, and I know he must have felt the heat of Dede's ambition.

Michael, John, Dede, Jim, and I went to work inventing the auction house that could beat Sotheby's at its own game. The ideas that emerged from these brainstorming sessions directed the business strategy that would dramatically increase Sotheby's sales. Looking at the decade of the 1980s, Sotheby's auction sales increased five-fold from $573 million in the 1979–80 season to $3.2 billion in the 1989–90 season. I believe we propelled the entire art market—auction houses and dealers—to extraordinary new heights. When it came to developing centers, the Taubman Company had always taken into account external and interior design, image, branding, and an understanding of retailing psychology. The same would hold true at Sotheby's. And just as our malls had challenged the insular department stores that crushed competition and controlled the distribution of brands, we aimed to bring new retail customers into a closed industry in which a relatively few individuals had been distributing the spoils.

Initially, there were small, subtle changes. We dropped the Parke-Bernet identity (the company had been called Sotheby Parke Bernet since the acquisition), and simplified the name to "Sotheby's." The subtext "Established 1744" was added to the logo to underscore our venerable history. We redesigned the auction catalogs printed for each sale, establishing a single worldwide graphic standard with much larger type. The 9-point type we had been using was too small to read for anyone old enough to afford fine art!

I immediately saw there were opportunities to dramatically improve the physical space at several Sotheby's office and auction facilities. Apparently, I made quite an impression on the Sotheby's staff in London when I took a practical but admittedly unorthodox approach to space planning. Author Robert Lacey in *Sotheby's: Bidding for Class* writes:

> Graham Llewellyn [Sotheby's UK CEO], knew that Alfred Taubman had taken control of Sotheby's when he glanced out of his office window one day and saw the considerable bulk of his new American boss teetering precariously on the roof. Taubman was looking down at the jumble of chimneys and roof extensions that reflected the auction house's growth over the years. Flow had been the secret of his success in the mall business, and he made the redesign and reordering of New Bond Street's rabbit warrens one of his first priorities.

On one of my less acrobatic space-planning tours of the New Bond Street facilities I noticed that there was a little-used storage room off the lobby. Although it had a very low ceiling, the space was perfect for a café to enliven the lobby and create a more welcoming feel to Sotheby's historic front door. We raised the ceiling, added a kitchen on the level below the lobby, and installed a motorized dumbwaiter to deliver orders to the café. A simple video system allowed the kitchen and waitstaff to communicate effectively.

Shortly before we opened for business, I received a call from a senior Sotheby's executive in London. He was nearly hysterical and was concerned that our café looked too much like—perish the thought—a *French* café, one you might see on the streets of Paris! That was exactly the look we were after, and I assured him that our café would fit right in and be attractive to people from all over the world. And that's precisely what happened. The Café (which is what we unimaginatively named it) was an instant hit. Clients stayed longer, staff held small meetings over lunch, visitors stopped in for tea and discovered Sotheby's for the first time. We introduced a lobster sandwich on brioche bread (a London first) that put our simple but distinctive cuisine on the map.

To further improve the customer experience in our London facilities we doubled the size of the main auction room and created a corridor that connected through the building from New Bond Street to Conduit Street. This helped rationalize the pedestrian flow and brought all departments together.

In New York we added skyboxes in the main auction room to add capacity and offer privacy for consignors and bidders preferring a lower profile. More importantly, we broke down the barriers between our people and our merchandise. In New York, most of the goods were stored away, out of sight in a warehouse uptown, which was hardly the ideal venue for looking at fine art. So we added six floors to our converted Kodak warehouse on York Avenue to create a ten-story, 400,000-square-foot complex where our experts could work in close proximity to the artwork, and where clients could easily view whatever was coming up for sale. Building a new headquarters also helped create synergies. Once the renovation was completed, in spring 2000, a client visiting to meet with the jewelry expert might pass by the furniture department and see the perfect side table for her living room. We opened up the interior space to put essentially everything on view. The new facility also features fantastic exhibition and sales space.

To expose our sales to an international audience we expanded the use of traveling exhibitions, which allowed potential bidders in Japan and Germany to view items that would be coming up for sale in New York or London. By making better use of our sixty offices around the world, we built larger audiences of bidders and consignors. We also formed an international advisory board to strengthen global relationships and fine-tune our client services. Assisting us were such respected business and cultural leaders as Baron Hans Heinrich Thyssen-Bornemisza de Kászon from Switzerland, Seiji Tsutsumi from Japan, the Honourable Sir Angus Ogilvy from the UK, Ann Getty from the U.S.A., Giovanni Agnelli from Italy, and the Infanta Pilar de Borbón, Duchess of Badajoz, from Spain.

We reallocated our marketing dollars away from institutional advertising to public relations and our client services staff. Our press office, strengthened by the hiring of Diana Phillips in 1985, created excitement and buzz surrounding the sales, and the client services staff was the heart and soul of our point-of-purchase marketing efforts. We also developed promotional programs to increase the number of subscribers to our catalogs and publications. Sotheby's *Preview,* a glossy magazine highlighting upcoming sales, profiling experts and clients, and celebrating the joys of collecting was significantly upgraded and transformed into an advertiser-supported publication. The thinking behind these moves, and behind much of our efforts at Sotheby's, was relatively simple. Auctions can be elegant and highly efficient ways of selling goods, anything from Pez dispensers to Treasury bonds. But they work best—they get the largest possible price for the seller—only if there are a large number of bidders.

To make sure I could sleep at night, we discontinued the sale of shrunken human heads, elephant tusks, and Nazi memorabilia. We also created an international art registry with the participation of law enforcement agencies around the world to help recover stolen art and limit the market for fakes and forgeries.

To retain and reward our talented people we introduced a phantom stock option program, giving more employees a stake in the company for the first time. Sotheby's had never had a problem attracting bright people, but many experts came to Sotheby's for training and then went on to become art dealers. Offering stock to our key people dramatically improved our retention, but since we were a private company it was difficult to objectively value the stock. It was primarily for this reason that we took the company public in 1987. The stock initially traded on both the American and London stock exchanges, and Sotheby's shares began trading on the New York Stock Exchange in 1988. The success of Sotheby's shares and the generosity of our stock option program made a career in the art auction business more financially rewarding than it had ever been before.

No one inside or outside the organization challenged the validity of these important but subtle initiatives. The same couldn't be said of some of the more fundamental innovations, which aimed to shake some dust off a very sleepy and insular industry.

In our brainstorming sessions we discussed our three primary groups of customers: art dealers, museums, and individual collectors. We came to the conclusion that dealers were both customers—our most important customers—and competitors. Dealers accounted for more than two-thirds of our sales. This reality was one of the reasons, in my opinion, that our service mentality had been so lacking. Professional dealers required far less hand-holding, promotion, and follow-through than individual buyers. They came to exhibitions with their clipboards in hand and dispassionately inspected and assessed the goods. At auction they bid with the same discipline and detachment. Essentially, they were superconfident customers looking for inventory to buy at wholesale and mark up in their own shops, where they played the role of salesman and adviser to less confident retail buyers. They were rewarded for this service by higher margins, just as Neiman Marcus is rewarded for displaying and selling Polo tennis shirts at full price.

In a more negative light, dealers were also known to manipulate the auction process, forming illegal dealer rings. In what came to be called "the Wednesday lunch," a group of dealers would determine who would buy what at what price at an upcoming auction, and set a date for their own private auction after the sale. In this way the goods were divvied up among the ring at the expense of the consignor and the auction house. Certainly not all dealers were involved in this skullduggery, but it was pretty clear to us that this was a widespread practice. This collusion had the effect of making what should be the ultimate efficient market—an open auction—into an inefficient one.

Here's where serial vision came in. We didn't simply want to make existing auctions better. We wanted to change the nature of a hidebound and inefficient business, and make it better. Without turning off our critical dealer customers, we wanted to add some competition in the salesroom. After all, just as was the case in our centers, Sotheby's primary responsibility was to the person selling the goods. It was our job to create the most vibrant and exciting market possible in which they could showcase their merchandise. Passionate individual buyers would drive higher auction results and make it more difficult for dealers to control the process.

To help develop larger numbers of individual buyers and strengthen Sotheby's identity as an approachable, knowledgeable resource for collectors and connoisseurs, we invested in several areas of the business that had long been neglected. Sotheby's International Realty, Sotheby's Appraisal Company, Sotheby's Restoration, Sotheby's Educational Programs, and Sotheby's Financial Services were all given new leadership and support. It was in the area of financial services that we really ruffled some dusty feathers.

Art dealers historically had offered cash up front to sellers and extended terms to buyers. This was a tremendous advantage over the auction houses. Let's say your rich uncle Harry from Harrison left you a terrific sporting painting, a well-wrought tableau of hounds, horses, and hunters. While you are very proud of the piece, college tuition bills have just arrived, and you could use some cash. So you head into Manhattan to visit an art dealer specializing in sporting paintings and to visit Sotheby's.

In the old days, the inevitably charming dealer would inspect your painting (typically with enthusiasm and grace) and offer to buy it at a specific price. If the amount were agreeable to you, he would write you a check on the spot. And by the way, if you wanted to select something to replace the painting, the dealer would sell it to you on credit, allowing you to pay off the purchase over several years. (This is how I purchased much of the art in my early collection.)

Sotheby's, on the other hand, would inspect the painting (perhaps with a bit less enthusiasm and grace), estimate what it might fetch at auction, and suggest that you place the painting in the next sale of sporting paintings, which could be as far off as six months. Even though the estimated sale price at auction could be twice the amount offered by the dealer, the uncertainty and wait at Sotheby's were deal breakers. We set out to change the rules of the game, and level the playing field by introducing conservative financing policies to both sellers and buyers. Under the new rules, we would inspect Uncle Harry's painting (with better manners), estimate its value at auction, and offer to write you a check for up to 50 percent of that amount. After the sale, we would send you an additional check for the balance—which had the potential to be significantly larger than the first payment, especially if we were to succeed in drawing more individual buyers to the auction room. Since a dealer is going to mark up the painting by 100 percent or more once he puts it in his window, our first check would probably be very close to the amount offered by the dealer. The second check would arrive from Sotheby's in a matter of months.

This tactic made us far more competitive in the quest for Uncle Harry's sporting painting. Dealers were forced to work a little harder and write larger checks, but we didn't see anything unfair about our financing policies. Another move we undertook to make the Sotheby's experience more customer-friendly was more controversial. Christie's and Sotheby's had a longstanding practice of extending credit to dealers. But as we were reimagining the auction business as a luxury retail business, Sotheby's decided to do the same thing that many of my department stores had done: help our customers finance their purchase. When we began offering credit on a larger, more formal scale to *individual buyers,* the Seurat hit the fan.

Foul, cried the art dealers' associations. Reckless, reported the art world press. To drive home their arguments against auction house financing, dealers and reporters hit upon the sale at Sotheby's of Vincent van Gogh's *Irises* on November 11, 1987. Put up for auction by John Whitney Payson, *Irises* was purchased by Australian businessman Alan Bond for $49 million ($53.9 million including the buyer's commission), at the time a record price for any work of art. John Marion, who was at the podium that evening in New York, captured the drama of those historic few in his book, *The Best of Everything:*

> Before long there was spirited bidding between two collectors on telephones manned by Sotheby's staffers. I felt like a referee in a tennis match as the bid bounced from one phone to the other: Forty-seven million now. Forty-eight million for it. Forty-nine million dollars now. I have forty-nine million dollars against you in the center . . . will you say fifty? At forty-nine million then on the far phone. At forty-nine million then. All done . . . you still there? Fair warning. Sold! For forty-nine million.

The room exploded with applause, but the art world grumbled in protest. Many believed that because we extended credit to Bond, the price was somehow illegitimate and would artificially inflate the market. Never mind that we extended credit to dealers all the time. And never mind the fact that dealers arranged credit for buyers all the time.

Several months later, when Bond ran into financial trouble and was having difficulty paying us back on schedule, there were more breathless headlines. But the situation also demonstrated the appropriateness and conservative nature of our financing policies. At the first sign of trouble, we took possession of the painting, which was always available to us as collateral. Bond consigned several other paintings from his collection to cover his obligations. And in 1990 we sold *Irises* a second time for a substantial commission to the Getty Museum, where it hangs to this day, overlooking the Pacific Ocean in Malibu.

In fact, *Irises* was one of the most profitable objects ever represented by Sotheby's. But the controversy was so great, we discontinued the practice of accepting the object being bid on as collateral and decided not to lend on any art within twelve months of purchase. We did, however, continue to take bids on credit and offer advanced payments to sellers following very conservative lending practices. Mitchell Zuckerman, who is president of Sotheby's Financial Services, has done a great job of making financing a dependable and significant competitive tool and income stream for the company. His loan portfolio performs year in and year out with a minuscule default rate.

But financing wasn't the only Sotheby's initiative that came under fire unfairly. Sotheby's had a venue called the Arcade, where items of more modest cost—principally decorative art, furniture, and collectibles—were offered for sale. Buyers could get a bargain on a beautiful dining room set, classic stemware and flatware, or garden statues. Before I became involved, lots were exhibited for the convenience of the dealers. If there were twenty dining room tables in the sale, the tables were all together in one area of the exhibition space. Chairs were in a separate area reserved just for chairs, even if they matched the tables. The place looked like a flea market, but the dealers, clipboards in hand, didn't mind sorting dispassionately through the inventory. But for individual buyers, this arrangement was a veritable wall of threshold resistance

As Milton Petrie and Leslie Wexner knew, I had some pretty firm ideas about how best to design shopping areas in a way that broke down barriers between customers and the merchandise. I thought we should arrange the dining tables and chairs in room settings. We might even place flatware, dishes, and stemware from the sale on the table—the way people use these beautiful items in their homes. Side tables were placed beside an heirloom headboard on a colorful Heriz carpet. On the walls were framed mirrors, prints, and paintings. We carried this display technique over to our catalogues as well.

As you might guess, individual buyers found the groupings helpful in making their buying decisions, and attendance at our Arcade auctions increased dramatically. But the art world was furious. I was accused of turning Sotheby's into Bloomingdale's. This guy from Detroit, who had already destroyed downtowns the country over with his huge malls, was "malling" the art world. He was hanging mirrors on walls and placing chairs with tables! Of course, what we were doing was breaking down threshold resistance. Competition and new ideas were shining rays of light into their secretive, exclusive, largely unregulated world. And the art world was not happy.

What's more, we were reaching out to new collectors through high-profile, unapologetically glamorous celebrity sales. We made history with the 1987 sale of the jewels of the Duchess of Windsor in Geneva, Switzerland (at which Elizabeth Taylor successfully bid $623,333 by phone from Beverly Hills for the duchess's plume-shaped "Prince of Wales" diamond brooch); the 1996 sale of the property of the late Jacqueline Kennedy Onassis (at which the publisher of *Cigar*

Aficionado magazine purchased a presidential humidor for $574,500); and the ten-day-long sale of the Andy Warhol Collection in 1988 (at which the artist's collection of store-bought cookie jars went for $247,000).

Such extravaganzas, which would have been shunned as down-market by Sotheby's and Christie's before we came along, were fun, and made news around the world. More importantly, they got people interested in the auction experience and collecting. They also helped strengthen the business of dealers and retailers. After the Windsor sale, jewelers saw a dramatic increase in the sales of estate and antique jewelry. Long before eBay came along, news of the prices fetched for Warhol's everyday possessions set off a tidal wave of collecting interest in everything from baseball cards to *Star Wars* memorabilia. Charities and other nonprofit institutions began to feature auctions in their annual fund-raising activities. Interior decorators saw an upswing in client interest in antiques and original art for their homes and offices. Americans, historically averse to saving anything, ran to their attics in search of comic books, record albums, and vintage clothing (a collecting category introduced with great success at Sotheby's by my stepdaughter, Tiffany).

Looking back, I really believe we played a pivotal role in this revolution that has brought joy to millions and great success to every sector of the art market. My good friend Bill Acquavella, one of the most respected art dealers, says that he and his industry colleagues all benefited from Sotheby's tactics that were attacked as unfair and unfriendly. Most people came along begrudgingly as the numbers spoke for themselves. Our rivals at Christie's railed against every innovation or new policy we introduced, only to adopt or imitate our practices within a few months.

A golfing buddy recently told me an interesting story about the initial reaction of professional golfers to the ascension of Tiger Woods. The young superstar certainly shook up the clubby, insular world of the PGA in all sorts of ways when he burst onto the scene in 1996. Not only was he one of the most talented players ever to explode onto the scene—in others words, better—he was different. He kept in superb physical shape and approached the game with extraordinary intensity. Many old-timers were threatened by Tiger, even though he appealed to a far broader audience and brought new commercial and popular attention to the tour. The established pros didn't want him in their club.

Today, the better players are matching Tiger's work ethic and much of the resentment has faded. Why? Because everybody's ship has been lifted. In 1995, the year before Tiger, just nine golfers won a million dollars or more on the PGA tour. In 2005, seventy-eight golfers were million-dollar money winners! Television revenues are up—and so are the purses at tournaments. Golf courses are being built at record pace, manufacturers of golf equipment are enjoying record sales, and golf tournaments can't handle the crowds of spectators, young and old.

Now, I'm no Tiger Woods. His long game is much better than mine. But his story, and the saga of Sotheby's barrier-busting innovations, stand as cautionary tales for any business leader or marketer. Broadening audiences and intensifying competition usually helps industries and every talented, hard-working participant in them. Ignore the cries of entrenched individuals frightened by change.

I suppose some in the art world, who still long for the closed, noncompetitive world before Windsor, Warhol, and Onassis, will never get over it. But thanks to the ideas that came out of those initial brainstorming sessions at Sotheby's, there's a whole lot less resistance standing between customers and the enriching world of art, antiques, and collectibles.

I feel good about that, and so should everybody at Sotheby's.

~ TWELVE ~

Selling Art and Root Beer

It's always interesting to spend time with college students. They ask great questions and hang on every word of your answers. In 1985 I got a call from a professor at the Harvard Business School asking if I would come to campus to discuss my "eclectic" business experience. He said the students and faculty would be particularly interested in any common threads running through the seemingly unrelated fields of retailing, real estate, art, restaurants, and professional sports (I had recently become the majority owner of the Michigan Panthers football team of the new United States Football League).

I was flattered by the invitation—this was Harvard, after all—and went right to work crafting my half-hour "lecture." It was a great opportunity for me to examine my businesses and achievements from a fresh point of view. Since my schoolday afternoons at Sims department store, I had spent little time reflecting on my career, let alone the underlying principles guiding the decisions, risks, and investments I had made as an adult. Other than my involvement, what did Taubman shopping centers, A&W Restaurants, Sotheby's, Woodward & Lothrop, and the Panthers have in common? Good question.

To get the students' attention and set up my central themes, I led with a provocative introduction:

> How can one find even the thinnest of common threads running through the worlds of fine art, football, root beer, fashion, and real estate? You may find there's more similarity in the challenge of marketing a precious painting by Degas and a frosted mug of root beer than you ever thought possible.

Before examining my individual companies and the industries in which they operated, I offered these four personal precepts for consideration:

1. Our consumer society, not driven by the satisfaction of basic needs, is fueled by the fantasy, flight, and excitement of a possible purchase. People will buy—on impulse—products and services they feel will make them happier.
2. You can sell almost anything once. But repeat business is built on consumer confidence, perceived quality and value, excitement, a rich mix of customer opportunities, as well as convenience and service.
3. The biggest mistake you can make is to price your product or plan your development based on what others are doing, rather than on how you see the opportunity. Study the consumer. Work for that part of the market that's there for the taking, with a creative new idea or an old idea made better, not just different.
4. Become an expert in one fundamental area of your market or business. No one starts out as a generalist. In my case, I started as a store planner and learned the basics of successful retail design. Through that discipline, I sharpened my understanding of the customer.

The lecture hall and the curious faces of the bright students and distinguished faculty members inspired me to new levels of philosophic thought. I went on to observe:

> In retailing and entertainment you are not just satisfying a need. A shopping trip involves fantasy and fun. In fact, the purchase is often secondary to the experience. If people lived just for necessity, we wouldn't have the mature consumer markets we have today. Retailing and most other businesses are far more than delivery systems of needed goods and services. Success comes through motivation and invention.
>
> Consider "need." I know that you've learned in the course of your studies that business success has to do with "satisfying needs." Find a need and fill it. But I submit that there is no need in this country for another store, restaurant, or television program. There is no need for another mall or football team. Nobody has to own a Degas painting. When you're thirsty, you don't have to frost your mug and fill it with root beer. You don't capture a consumer market anymore by solving a basic need. Most people above the poverty level in America just don't need anything. Winning businesses go beyond needs satisfaction, offering joy, pleasure and entertainment. Certainly mine do.

Here, I knew I was challenging one of the basic precepts of business school curricula. For generations, business textbooks had taken the reader step by step through the process of identifying a need and designing a business to address it. But by the late twentieth century, there was far more to business than satisfying basic needs. The pony express and Federal Express both represent systems of delivering mail and packages. The former filled a basic need; the latter introduced levels of speed and efficiency we never knew we needed. And what's that speed and efficiency worth? Well, you pay 39¢ to send a letter through the U.S. mail or up to $45 to have that same letter delivered overnight by FedEx. Clearly, going beyond mere needs satisfaction can pay handsome dividends. By upgrading the beans, training excellent people, and creating a welcoming environment, Starbucks charges big bucks for a cup of coffee!

So we examined the customer appeal of Sotheby's, Woodies, Taubman malls, and A&W. But the class really wanted to know more about the logic behind the new United States Football League (USFL), the spring football experiment of which the Michigan Panthers were inaugural members. The world certainly did not "need" spring-summer professional football. There was plenty of football on television during the fall, and the Super Bowl drew international audiences in the hundreds of millions. In the spring-summer, fans seemed perfectly happy with the other sports and activities on offer.

But television advertisers longed for more television sports aimed at men 18–54 years old, especially in the spring and early summer months after the end of the hockey, basketball, and football seasons. There was no NASCAR on TV to speak of in those days, and golf, in its pre-Tiger era, had limited appeal. So only baseball provided content over the summer for the companies advertising to guys who drink beer, chew tobacco, use razor blades, and buy cars (which sell best in the spring and summer months).

I love football, especially University of Michigan football. No sports experience comes close to matching the atmosphere at a Michigan vs. Ohio State game in front of 110,000 screaming fans in Michigan Stadium on a crisp fall Saturday afternoon in Ann Arbor (especially if the Wolverines win). So I was interested in 1982 when a friend from Detroit, Judge Peter Spivak, introduced me to the concept for the USFL. Judge Spivak served as the league's first president before ESPN executive Chet Simmons was named commissioner. Chet successfully negotiated network television contracts with ESPN and ABC.

Each team would operate under a reasonable annual salary cap (initially just $1.8 million) and control drafting rights to players from nearby colleges. In other words, a Michigan franchise would end up with a number of fan favorites from the University of Michigan and Michigan State University. Because our league would be active after the NFL season, stadium facilities were available. In the past, I had thought about buying a professional baseball team (I had explored purchases of the Baltimore Orioles and the Detroit Tigers). The Panthers would be different but still fun. They would play in the Pontiac Silverdome (then home to the Detroit Lions), which was just a few minutes from the home I was born in, on Ottawa Drive. Along with my friend and fellow college football fan Max Fisher—Max, who had attended Ohio State on a football scholarship, sat with me at just about every Ohio State–Michigan game for thirty-years—I took the plunge.

We never thought we would make a lot of money. But we did hope to have some fun. Our first season, in 1983, started out miserably. Before we knew it, we were 1–4, tied for last in the league. Detroit-area fans are very loyal, but we were testing their patience and dampening their enthusiasm for spring football. You have to remember that the Lions had not fielded much of a team for many years (they still haven't). We had to do something, or even more of the Silverdome's 80,000 seats would be empty.

In desperation, I asked Shire Rothbart, my trusted, talented finance guy who helped convert all those ground leases on the Irvine Ranch, to take over operations for the Panthers. I wanted to win, and Shire, who had no football or sports experience, was a smart, competitive guy with a knack for finding creative solutions to difficult problems. The first call he made after learning about his new assignment was to an agent he had been introduced to at one of our earlier games.

"What's keeping the Panthers from winning some games?" asked Shire.

The agent said we had a good coach and good players at the skilled positions, but a lousy offensive line. "You can't win if you don't give [quarterback] Bobby Hebert time to throw to [star receiver] Anthony Carter. Shire, I'd go out and get some new tackles and guards."

"Where do I get them?"

"For the last few years, the Pittsburgh Steelers have fielded the best offensive line in football. They've got a lot of depth at those positions. We might be able to sign a couple of those guys. Who knows?"

Shire made a few calls, and before the sixth game of the season we assembled a new-look offensive line, complete with three former Pittsburgh Steelers: Tyrone McGriff, Ray Pinney, and Thom Dornbrook. We won our next six games, put as many as 60,000 fans in the Silverdome seats, made the playoffs, and defeated the Philadelphia Stars (owned by developer Myles Tanenbaum) 24–22 in the first-ever USFL championship game in Denver's Mile High Stadium. The deciding 48-yard touchdown pass was thrown by Bobby Hebert, who was given plenty of time in the pocket by our offensive line, to Anthony Carter with three minutes remaining in the game. Shire's buddy was right. Nobody "needed" another football team, but we were having lots of fun, and so were the sports fans in Detroit.

One great story I'll never forget took place during the off-season after our championship victory. Our head of personnel at the Taubman Company, Tom Bithell, came up with a terrific program to offer Panthers to local high school football teams as assistant coaches—at no cost to the high schools—during the fall. This kept our guys out of trouble and gave youngsters the opportunity to learn from gifted professional athletes. After Tom presented the program to the Panthers at an all-team meeting, his assistant received a phone call from a player who had been unable to make the meeting but wanted to sign up.

"No problem," said Tom's assistant. "Just give me your number, and I'll have Tom call you back."

"Great," responded the player. "My number is 54."

• • •

As it turned out, our fun was short-lived. The league began to unravel when the majority of the other owners voted to abandon our unique spring schedule, shift to the fall in 1986, and compete directly against the NFL. They initiated a lawsuit challenging the NFL's monopolistic hold on professional football. While we prevailed in court—winning damages of just $3—no merger ever took place. My friend Donald Trump, who joined the league in September of 1983 as owner of the New Jersey Generals, was an enthusiastic supporter of the fall schedule. He also blew through the team's salary cap and the USFL's unique economic structure with the signing of players like Heisman Trophy winner Doug Flutie. I like and respect Donald very much, but in his youth he could be a bit impatient.

We hired Vince Lombardi Jr., son of the legendary Green Bay Packers coach, as president of the Panthers to allow Shire to return to his financial duties. Vince was a terrific guy, but the league was imploding all around us. My beloved Panthers played out the last season in California as the Oakland Invaders. Bobby Hebert and Anthony Carter went on to have standout careers in the NFL with the New Orleans Saints and Minnesota Vikings respectively. And Max and I came away with a clearer understanding of how to make a small fortune: start with a large fortune and buy a football team.

It's important not simply to learn from failure, but to look beyond it. Neither the Harvard Business School class nor I knew it at the time, but the ill-fated USFL would demonstrate the appetite for professional football in markets the conservative, stingy NFL had always ignored. Today's Jacksonville, Arizona, Tennessee, and Carolina franchises would probably not have come to pass so soon without the surprising success of the USFL in those markets. And many of the USFL's innovations have been adopted by the NFL, including the two-point conversion option after touchdowns and the coach's challenge utilizing instant replay.

In the Q & A period following my remarks, students and faculty zeroed in on the concept of going beyond needs satisfaction. We talked about the importance of the salesperson, the opportunity to assist customers lacking confidence, the critical role of service and convenience, the advantage of adding a touch of theater to your presentation, and the critical nature of the shopping experience. By the end of the hour, I think they all found more similarity in the challenge of marketing a frosted mug of root beer and a precious painting by Degas then they had ever thought possible.

But all was not well. I'm a visual guy. And in the portion of my slide show on Sotheby's I had featured a Modigliani painting, *The Dreamer,* which was being offered in our November sale of impressionist and modern paintings. The painting, which depicted a reclining female nude, would later sell for $4.62 million in New York. Apparently, a woman in the class was offended by the painting, and complained to the professor that she had been made to feel uncomfortable and wanted an apology from me. Fortunately, a number of her fellow students convinced the sensitive young woman that she might need to broaden her acceptance of art and develop a thicker skin before she left Harvard Business School for the rough-and-tumble world of business.

More problematic, however, was the subsequent coverage of my talk in the *Wall Street Journal.* The paper didn't mind the Modigliani. But it was taken aback by my reference to root beer and art in the same sentence. Of course, rather than present the entire thought in context, the reporter (who had not heard the lecture) simply condensed it to read: "Selling art is like selling root beer." The A&W folks applauded the assertion, but the art world collectively gasped in shock and indignation (again). This was even worse than allowing dining room chairs to be displayed before auction in the general vicinity of the tables they were designed to complement! It got worse. Subsequent third- and fourth-hand journalistic accounts of the quote all over the world—in multiple languages—shorthanded and distorted the meaning even more. Within weeks of my triumphant Harvard lecture, my words had been distilled by the press to their ultimate clarity—"Art is root beer"—thus giving a whole new meaning to the term "pop art."

Some journalists came to my defense. For every commentator who found the phrase offensive, several others considered it profound. No one, unfortunately, was interested in the actual quote. This became abundantly clear when a business magazine staffer called to fact-check the "art is root beer" version. Our public relations office pointed out the error and sent the text of the lecture, highlighting the sentence "You may find there's more similarity in the challenge of marketing a frosted mug of root beer and a precious painting by Degas than you ever thought possible." The fact-checker called back to let us know that the shorter version of the quote would go into the publication, explaining, "Yours just doesn't sing."

With this attitude toward "fact-checking," heroic pronouncements such as "Give me liberty or give me death" could actually have been something like, "Let me take the liberty to ask you folks to reconsider the rather harsh sentence you have imposed." Who knows?

Well, at least the students and professors at Harvard knew what I meant. The best business opportunities in a mature consumer society deliver goods, services, and experiences that go beyond satisfying needs. Acquiring a precious Degas painting for your collection is a privilege and a joy. Enjoying a frosted mug of root beer at an A&W drive-in restaurant on a hot summer evening is a delight. Finding just the right dress for a special occasion makes you feel good about yourself. And watching Anthony Carter catch a game-winning touchdown pass is a memory that lasts a lifetime among friends.

Nobody needs to do any of these things. But companies profit by creating and delivering such opportunities. Businessmen and businesswomen who deliver such enjoyable experiences to their customers will win in today's mature, competitive markets. And you can quote me on that.

~ THIRTEEN ~

Going Public

In the 1980s, the trajectory of my career shifted somewhat. I was in my sixties, approaching the age at which many people retire. Because I was well-off, because my company had grown to be very large, and because I had become involved with highly publicized ventures, such as the Irvine Ranch and the Michigan Panthers, I had become something of a public figure, which was not what I had sought. As a result, a lot of opportunities were presented to me, and I pursued many of them. In retrospect, I probably would have been better off just building centers. But I was always fascinated with doing interesting things.

Taubman Centers was the heart of my business and my identity. I wasn't bored with developing centers. In the 1980s, we were still building, though not at the feverish pace of the late 1960s and early 1970s. In the mid-1970s, the dynamics of development had changed. Land costs had increased in the suburbs, and we believed the great wave of population growth in the outlying regions was beginning to slow. And so we began to look for opportunities in the more densely developed areas in between the first-generation shopping centers (downtowns) and second-generation shopping centers (regional malls). While the land was generally difficult to assemble, these locations offered great advantages: a 360-degree market, excellent road access, and large populations. We still held true to our old maxim that people shop where they live. But by building in more densely populated areas, we could also tap into people who were interested in shopping where they worked, too. And as we focused more on higher-end stores—and higher-end consumers—these locations made a great deal of sense. Applying many of the same principles and practices we had perfected with our large malls, we began to adapt them to somewhat different and smaller configurations. Of the nine properties we opened in the 1980s, four were done in urban locations.

Built in the late 1950s, the Mall at Short Hills, in northern New Jersey, was a poorly designed mess. The Prudential Insurance Company, which owned the property, in the late 1970s asked us to look into redeveloping it, which we did. After we reopened it in 1980, it quickly turned into what one writer called a center "for all-stars."

In 1982, in partnership with my great friend Sheldon Gordon, we opened the eight-floor Beverly Center in Los Angeles, which was our first real attempt at vertical retailing. The site was only nine acres, much smaller than our typical development. But with two hundred specialty stores, a Hard Rock Cafe, and movie theaters, it quickly emerged as a destination for many of the 2 million people who lived within a fifteen-minute drive. The same year, we opened Stamford Town Center in Stamford, Connecticut. Again, it was smaller than most of our superregional centers: 900,000 square feet built on eleven acres. In 1984, its third year of operation, the Stamford Town Center reported sales of $300 per square foot, which, I noted at the time, was like a rookie baseball player batting average. Thanks to the growing wealth and job creation in these near-in suburban areas, these centers today are among our most successful, with some of the highest sales-per-square-foot figures in the industry. Today, the Mall at Short Hills has five specialty department stores: Bloomingdale's, Saks,

Macy's, Nordstrom, and Neiman Marcus. And the stores do a tremendous volume—over $1,000 per square foot in sales. Last year, the 8,000-square-foot Tiffany store did almost as much in sales as a department store.

In Charleston, South Carolina, we created Charleston Place, a hotel, conference, and shopping complex in the heart of one of America's most historic downtowns. Gifted architect John Carl Warnecke assisted us with the design. Located at the intersection of King Street and Market Street—the city's primary retail thoroughfares—Charleston Place's shops were carefully designed to enliven (actually, rescue) the struggling street-level retail that existed at the time. Mayor Joseph P. Riley Jr., who brought us to town, is still in office and justifiably brags about the new businesses and economic vitality spawned by Charleston Place. Mayor Riley provided the leadership to convince local entrepreneurs to invest downtown, and today Charleston is a bustling, beautiful place to live or visit. Farther up the Atlantic coast in Manhattan, we were partners with Solomon Equities in 712 Fifth Avenue.

Through all this growth, the Taubman Company remained very much a family company. Not everybody thinks it's a good idea to do business with family and friends. While I understand the reluctance, some of my most successful and rewarding business initiatives have involved my closest friends and family members. My first hire when I founded the Taubman Company was my father who worked with me until his death. Two of the company's three most senior officers today are my sons, Robert and William. My friends Max Fisher and Henry Ford II were partners in the Irvine Ranch and Sotheby's acquisitions. In fact, I can't remember a major business step I ever took without some involvement of family and friends.

Clearly, not all family businesses succeed. After all, not all families succeed. But there is plenty of evidence to suggest that there is something special about organizations imbued with a healthy dose of familial DNA. The cover story in the November 10, 2003, issue of *Business Week,* headlined "Family, Inc.," began with this introduction: "Surprise! One-third of the S&P 500 companies have founding families involved in management. And those are usually the best performers." Here's what the magazine reported:

> Forget the celebrity CEO. Look beyond Six Sigma and the latest technology fad. One of the biggest strategic advantages a company can have, it turns out, is blood lines. *Business Week* has found that a surprisingly large share of Corporate America—177 companies, or a third of the S&P 500—have founders or their families still on the scene, in most cases as directors or senior managers.
>
> And, in what may be Corporate America's biggest and best-kept secret, they're beating the pants off their nonfamily-run rivals.

That's not surprising to me. Although they may not be mandated by any Sarbanes-Oxley regulation, devotion, dedication, loyalty, and deep personal involvement are critical requirements of good corporate governance. It just makes sense that if the fate of my family name and fortune are directly linked with the business I'm running, my effort and commitment—in most cases—will exceed those of a "hired hand." Call it passion. Call it love. Call it survival. Family employees and leaders just have more skin in the game.

I like the fact that there's a Ford driving the future of Ford Motor Company (I personally witnessed and admired the intense pride and dedication of Henry Ford II during our decades of friendship). Founding families give their companies distinctive flavor and soul. That's not a bad thing. I had the pleasure and honor to sit on the board of directors of the Getty Oil Company in the 1970s and 1980s. The Getty family owned 40 percent of the stock, and the Sara B. Getty Foundation (the entity that created and supports the wonderful Getty Museum) owned 11 percent. Fellow board member Gordon Getty, the son of J. Paul Getty, would occasionally serenade us at board dinners with a full-blown aria. I'm not a great fan of opera, but I enjoyed these extemporaneous performances. They served to remind us that we were in a very real sense members of an extended family—a family that had a tremendous stake in the future of Getty Oil.

Sure, family feuds and bad seeds have taken their toll on family businesses. But more often than not, these organizations stay focused and grow. *Business Week* observed on 11/16/2003:

> With tight-knit family leaders at the top, decision-making can be easier and faster, allowing family corporations to pounce on opportunities others might miss. Their often paternalistic corporate cultures may lead to lower turnover and development of managerial talent. And unlike outside CEOs, family chief executives know that their families are in it for the long haul, making them more likely to reinvest in the business.

I've had good luck and more than my share of fun with family businesses—starting with my own. Part of the reason I was able to get involved with a range of activities in the 1980s was the strength of the team running the Taubman Company. Bob Larson, who is now at Lazard, was president and a gifted leader. And my two sons, Bob and Bill, were both there. I had hoped they would come work for the company, but I didn't presume they would. They were both intelligent young men and were always interested in what I was doing. And while my schedule was always hectic, we did manage to spend quality time together.

In 1981, to celebrate William's graduation from Cambridge University, where he had earned an advanced degree in philosophy and religion, fourteen of us were among the first westerners to gain entry to Tibet after cold-war tensions had cooled. It was an interesting group. Joining me and a young woman I was dating at the time, were

Max and Marjorie Fisher; New York attorney Peter Tufo and his mother; Italian businessman Emilio Gioia and his wife, Iris; my attorney and friend Jeffrey Miro and his wife, Marsha; my daughter, Gayle, and her husband, Michael; Dr. Ralph Brandt; and William. I had sponsored a mission to China for a number of United States mayors. In return, the government of China had invited us to tour their fascinating country.

A highlight of the trip was a visit to an industry exposition in Guangzhou, or Canton, at the time the most important trading center in south China. On display were the newest products of China's emerging economy. I was particularly impressed with a manufactured terrazzo tile as good as any sold in Italy and less than a quarter of the cost. The Taubman Company bought floor tile by the thousands of square feet. This stuff was first-rate and cheap. My son-in-law, Michael, who is a microsurgeon, was equally excited about a medical microscope priced at around $7,500. The German equivalent sold for more than $45,000. We had every intention of placing orders. But when we met with the senior trade officials we were informed that the piece of terrazzo I held in my hand and the microscope Michael had admired were the only ones in existence. They had no intention of selling their "display" samples.

When my sons began working in the company, they never reported to me. Bobby started in our Washington office working under Bob Larson, doing land work. He then moved to San Francisco and ultimately ran the leasing department on the West Coast, and then I brought him to Detroit. He was named president in 1990 and is today also chairman and chief executive officer. William worked in investment banking for Oppenheimer a few years and came to work for the company in 1984. Today, he's chief operating officer.

I've also enjoyed my involvement in the Athena Group, a private nonretail real estate development firm I started in 1995 with my stepdaughter Tiffany's husband. We've completed successful residential and office projects as close as Washington, D.C., and Manhattan, and as far away as Moscow and the city of Baku in the oil-rich republic of Azerbaijan (formerly part of the Soviet Union). In Baku we transformed a six-story structure built by the Germans in 1906 as a mill and wheat storage facility into a modern office building. The handsome exterior of the building (the brick walls were four feet thick to survive earthquakes) was designed to blend into the urban fabric of Baku, masking its original function. Much of the interior was essentially a massive, open silo, so we had to add the floors. Because the soil was inadequate to handle the weight, we designed a truss system at the roofline from which we actually hung the floors. In order to convince the city's planning board to allow windows on the sixth floor—which was the original attic space—one of our associates, Metin Negrin, flew to Paris to photograph top-story dormer window treatments throughout the city. We were convincing enough, and the sixth-floor tenants today pay top dollar for fabulous views of the Caspian Sea.

Our building, which was the first "class A" office building in Baku, leased up immediately to major international oil companies. On street level, HSBC Bank and British Airways occupied the retail space. While record keeping and accounting procedures are far from perfect in Azerbaijan, we got our money back on the project in just eighteen months and are still partners in the very successful building.

Longstanding friends continued to be a great source of new ideas and businesses. I met Dixon Boardman in the 1970s when he was an investment adviser with Kidder, Peabody in New York. He did a great job for me, and we became good friends and golf partners. After Kidder went through a series of acquisitions by General Electric and Paine Webber, I suggested that Dixon start a hedge fund, actually, a fund of funds. He was excited about the idea, and with an initial investment of $22 million (of which $10 million was mine) created the Optima Fund in 1988. Today, Dixon's fund manages about $6 billion, and we're still the best of friends.

With the assistance of my friend Mort Zuckerman, an accom-

plished real estate developer and publisher of *U.S. News & World Report,*
the Athena Group invested in Russia's first independent tabloid
newspaper. The editor was a talented journalist named Artyom Borovik, who also hosted the nation's most popular television news
program, a *60 Minutes*-style show. Encouraging and facilitating the
development of a free press in Russia was heady stuff. But our involvement ended abruptly when Artyom was killed in a very suspi-
cious private airplane accident.

This was not my first exposure to a family-owned media business.
I owned a small media company headquartered in Phoenix, Arizona,
in the 1970s. And in 1986, I pursued an investment in the Pulitzer
Publishing Company, a very successful family-owned and -operated
business. The deal was brought to me by Felix Rohatyn, a partner in
the investment firm Lazard Frères. Flush with cash from the divest-
ment of the Irvine Ranch and a major investment in the Taubman
Company portfolio by the General Motors Pension Trust, I asked
Felix to keep his eyes open for promising opportunities.

The Pulitzer Publishing Company was a terrific media conglomerate operating daily newspapers in St. Louis and Tucson, weeklies in
suburban Chicago, seven television stations, and two radio stations.
It was well run and very profitable (it still is). Four members of the
Pulitzer family, feeling that Joseph Pulitzer Jr., the patriarch of the
venerable family, was being stingy with their money, were looking
for someone to purchase their stakes in the company. Lazard was
representing them.

I was very interested in making an investment in Pulitzer on a
friendly basis. Regardless of Joseph's tight-fisted family relationships,
senior management was extremely capable. Hostile actions, which
rarely benefit anybody, are a lousy reaction to threshold resistance.
In an April 1986 edition of the *New York Times,* business reporter Albert
Scardino described an important component of my investment
philosophy:

Indeed, like a rich uncle, Taubman has a history of helping families in distress. But the families he helps are those who want to fend off hostile raiders and at the same time convert their stock in a privately held company into cash . . . "In making a deal of any kind, you have to place opportunities where they are accessible," he said this week. "Beyond that, you have to be sure that everyone can come out feeling he has been treated fairly and has obtained something of value."

We didn't end up owning an interest in the company, but we did help the disenchanted family members achieve a fairer value for their holdings and earned a $6 million payout from Lazard. We could have pressed our position (we had the absolute right to purchase the shares), but I did not want to be involved on a negative basis.

The Taubman Company by the mid-1980s was a well-oiled, highly sophisticated machine. We had developed a great deal of sophistication and were always doing many projects at once. In 1985, we completed a transaction with the pension funds of General Motors and AT&T, one of the largest real estate deals of its time, which valued our centers at $2 billion. This provided me with the confidence and resources to spend time on other projects: Sotheby's, A&W, the Michigan Panthers, and increasingly, philanthropy.

Through our more than fifty years of friendship, I learned many important lessons from Max Fisher. One of the most important was his personal take on philanthropy. Max was a brilliant, pragmatic guy. Most business leaders promote giving and civic involvement as a responsibility or obligation—something you have to do in response to your success. Many refer to it as "giving back."

Not Max. He saw philanthropy as an opportunity—a privilege you earn as you succeed in life. It's not something you have to do; it's something that you should want to do. There are great rewards and joys in helping others and making a difference in your community.

In 1982, Max Fisher and I were involved in the development of the

Riverfront Apartments, which at the time represented the first market-rate housing built in Detroit in twenty-five years. The eight hundred units (built in two phases) of the Riverfront Apartments weren't a big moneymaker. In fact, despite twelve years of generous tax abatements granted by the city—which were challenged by community leaders in an aggressive campaign captured on bumper stickers all over town reading "Tax Max and His Pal Al"—we lost more than $50 million. The costs associated with the former industrial site (including the need to drive pilings for the foundations) coupled with the inherent complexity of vertical construction made the residential space we were building twice as expensive as buildings in the suburbs, where the people we were marketing to lived. Unfortunately, to be competitive with the abundant suburban alternatives, we could only charge around $1 per square foot per month in rent. In real estate parlance, that's what you call a development that just won't "pencil."

But Detroit mayor Coleman Young—who counted Max and me among the few suburbanites he trusted—was a persuasive man and a tireless advocate for revitalized housing for his city. He believed, and Max and I agreed, that the apartments would serve as a catalyst for more residential development along the Detroit River. We were right. The project leased up well, demonstrating the market viability (if not profitability) of riverfront housing. Several other projects with river views followed. And as expensive as it turned out to be, Max and I were proud of our contribution to downtown Detroit's rebound, which has continued, in starts and stops, to this day.

Max understood that getting involved in things you think will make a difference also makes good business sense. Education has been a major focus of my civic involvement for as long as I can remember. For example, in 1980, I—along with Michigan governor Jim Blanchard, business leaders, and the presidents of our state's public universities—founded the Michigan Partnership for New Education. I served as the organization's chairman. We raised $48 million from the state, the private sector, and the universities (their contributions were in-kind) for this innovative public-private initiative to experiment with creative approaches to education and improve the way our K—12 public school teachers were trained.

Dr. Judith Lanier, who at the time was the dean of Michigan State University's College of Education, was our guiding light. MSU's education school was annually ranked as one of the finest in the nation, and Judy was highly respected as an innovator. She understood the need to allow new levels of competition and nontraditional thinking into the struggling world of public education.

Consider the fact that our nation's public and private universities are the envy of the world, yet a shocking percentage of our elementary, middle, and high schools are failing. Central to this disconnect is that higher education in this country is a fiercely competitive enterprise. If you've recently experienced the stress of having a young member of your family prepare to enter college, you know what I mean. Dozens of seductive college recruitment brochures arrive at your home in the mail each week. Consumers (students and parents) have a mind-boggling array of choices to consider. Recognizing the advantages of market competition, we encouraged, with the support of then—Michigan governor John Engler, the state's first charter school initiatives. In fact, in 1996, after the Michigan Partnership had completed its work, I cofounded and provided $35 million in financing for a charter school company called The Leona Group. Leona was named after the mother of cofounder William Coats. Bill was an experienced public school administrator and education professor, who had come to head the Michigan Partnership from a senior position with the Kellogg Foundation. This successful for-profit corporation today operates more than 50 charter schools in Michigan, Arizona, Indiana, and Ohio. Believe me, I understand the controversial nature of charter schools. But I remain convinced that without a healthy injection of market forces, our entrenched public school systems—especially in inner cities—will never embrace the necessary reforms.

The Michigan Partnership also pushed to allow the certification of nontraditional teachers, especially retired engineers from our state's world-class automotive companies. These mature, talented folks could excite students—both girls and boys—about math and science, subjects in which there was and still is a shortage of teachers.

Of course, "teaching the teachers" to make sure they were equipped with the latest and most effective techniques and understanding was another of our primary goals. While they are not compensated accordingly, teachers are among the most important professionals in our society. And they are very willing to invest their time in upgrading skills and employing tested new approaches to instruction. During a visit to Northern Michigan University in our state's beautiful Upper Peninsula (the university was kind enough to grant me an honorary degree), a public school teacher from a very rural district came up to me in tears, explaining that the training and support she had received from the Michigan Partnership for New Education had been the only professional enrichment she had experienced in her more than twenty-five years of teaching. Her sincere, emotional thanks was all the proof I needed that our efforts over the six years of the program's existence had been successful.

Beyond the personal rewards, why get involved? When companies have to spend billions of dollars providing remedial instruction in reading, simple math, and problem solving, that's a double tax. They've paid once for the failed school systems, and now they have to essentially create schools of their own to stay competitive with educated workforces around the world. The future success of every business, including the Taubman Company, depends on the quality of the workforce coming along.

In a 1990 address to the Greater Detroit Chamber of Commerce, I suggested that our great state of Michigan had been blessed in the late nineteenth and early twentieth centuries with a steady flow of immigrants to staff our assembly lines, build our roads, and bring new ideas to our businesses. But where was all this energy and capability going to come from as we looked ahead to the twenty-first century?

> Unlike the 1890s, our hope for the future will not be found on the deck of a ship crossing the Atlantic . . . but at a student's desk or computer terminal in a classroom in Detroit. For these "new immigrants" right here at home, their symbol of liberty is not a statue in New York Harbor . . . but a teacher beckoning young minds to learn. My friends, this state's and this nation's chances of surviving as a first-class industrial power will be determined by our ability to educate our young people. More than ever before, educated people will be our most important resource.

In the area of higher education I have also focused on the things that will influence the environment in which my businesses can operate successfully and my community can thrive. At the University of Michigan I provided leadership support for the medical library, the health care center, and the College of Architecture and Urban Planning, all of which bear my name. At Brown University and Michigan I helped develop interdisciplinary programs in American institutions and public policy to expose students to the workings of our great nation. And at Harvard's Kennedy School of Government, through the encouragement of my good friend and fishing buddy Dean Graham Allison, I established the Taubman Center for State and Local Government in 1990 to focus needed attention on the way our public and political institutions affect the way we live and work in America. Each year we send a number of Taubman Fellows from the Detroit area to attend the center's terrific summer programs for state and local officials from all over the nation. All we require of our Detroit fellows is that they share their experiences with us over lunch when they return from Cambridge.

Friends often inspire our philanthropy. New York senator Jacob Javits was a brilliant man and one of my favorite tennis partners.

Unfortunately, his life was cut short by the terrible degenerative condition known as amyotrophic lateral sclerosis (ALS), or Lou Gehrig's disease. I will never forget the last time I visited him in his Manhattan apartment in late 1985, a few months before he passed away. His mind was still razor sharp, but his body had shrunk nearly to the size of a doll. I vowed as I left him that day to do whatever I could to tackle this monstrous killer. Years later, I met Dr. Eva Feldman, a world-class neurologist and professor at the University of Michigan. In addition to being one of my physicians—a medical challenge in itself—Eva has done groundbreaking work in the area of ALS. It is an honor for me to be able to provide financial assistance for her work in memory of Jacob and all he did for New York and our country.

In 1979, the Michigan Cancer Foundation (one of the founding members of what today is the nationally recognized Barbara Ann Karmanos Cancer Institute) approached me with an urgent need. It seems they were close to losing a star researcher named Jerome Horwitz. Dr. Horwitz was being wooed by every cancer center in the country, and the foundation was concerned that if his research facilities were not upgraded immediately, he would move on. I agreed to pay for a fully equipped laboratory floor in a new medical building being developed on the campus of the Detroit Medical Center. They call it the A. Alfred Taubman Facility for Environmental Carcinogenesis Research. Dr. Horwitz stayed. And while he never came up with a cure for cancer, in that space with the long name he completed his groundbreaking, lifesaving research resulting in the development of azidothymidine, better known as AZT, the first drug approved by the Federal Drug Administration for the treatment of HIV infection and AIDS. Not bad.

Through my philanthropic efforts, and through the range of business ventures I became involved with, I became more of a public figure in the 1980s. But my most significant step in being more of a public figure—and in having more of my business be a matter of public interest—came in 1992. At the Taubman Company, our projects were getting larger, and there was concern about how to finance them. In addition, with the company having grown so large, the executives wanted to use publicly traded stock as a part of compensation. I had generally resisted taking the company public. Over the years, we had shown a great capability to finance projects. And I always preferred to own more of my projects, rather than less. What's more, aside from ceding a portion of control and making more of the business public knowledge, selling shares to the public would mean putting our fate in the hands of Wall Street analysts and money managers, who I felt never really understood the business of real estate. I didn't see a public offering as the culmination of a lifework. Nonetheless, in November 1992, we sold shares to the public. Here, again, the Taubman Company was an innovator. Before going public, we transformed the company into an umbrella partnership real estate investment trust (REIT, or UPREIT). This structure, in which the REIT doesn't directly own the properties, but rather a stake in an umbrella partnership that in turn owns interests in properties, allows for a more favorable tax treatment to founders like myself. We were the first UPREIT, and within a few years many other companies followed suit.

By the early 1990s, then, my private businesses and private life had been transformed. I served as chairman of two large publicly held companies (Sotheby's and Taubman Centers) was involved in many civic organizations, and had grown accustomed to seeing my name in print a great deal, although I was never totally comfortable with that. My net worth and the contents of my art collection were a matter of continual public speculation. Sure, I enjoyed the accolades and attention and the opportunities it presented. But I was to learn with Sotheby's that being a public figure involved with a highly public company could be a double-edged sword.

FOURTEEN

The Best and Worst of Times

On Tuesday, March 10, 1994, we celebrated the 250th anniversary of the founding of Sotheby's. The company's New Bond Street galleries never looked more festive as members of London society arrived to honor the venerable auction house on its birthday.

As chairman and majority owner of Sotheby's, I was called upon to deliver the toast to Sotheby's. The pomp and circumstance surrounding the dinner, described in a detailed agenda, let me know I was a long way from A&W. We greeted guests for a champagne reception in a receiving line. After a fanfare of trumpets, a single bagpiper led us up the stairs and through the building for an elegant dinner. At the end of dinner, a line of bagpipers marched slowly among the tables and assembled behind me. As the toastmaster cried out, "The Queen," an orchestra played the British national anthem. After the pipers marched out, it was my turn to speak.

Of the 250 years Sotheby's had been in business, I had been involved for just a bit more than a decade. But it had been a period of significant change, growth, and success. While the company's financial and market position had never been stronger, there were still some doubters who feared that American control would forever alter the character of this very British institution. This was my opportunity to put those fears to rest.

While I knew most of the people in the room, I had some reason to be concerned. I had not always done well with audiences beyond the borders of the United States. In 1987, while on the board of directors of the Chase Manhattan Bank, I was invited to address the leaders of the business community in Brazil. At the time, Brazil was attempting to get out from under billions of dollars of international debt (they were no longer paying principal or interest). The nation owed about $8 billion to a bank consortium that included Chase. I'm not sure why, but the officers of the bank thought I was just the guy to go down to Brasilia to encourage this struggling nation—rich in resources but short on political and economic stability—to make good on their obligations.

I was as diplomatic as I could be. But I did suggest that the nation's leaders consider "resuming productive relations with the international community, including negotiating an arrangement with the IMF and reconsidering the interest moratorium." I don't speak Portuguese. But I do know when I'm being chewed out in any language. Following what I thought was enthusiastic applause from the attendees, my host, Brazil's minister of finance, delivered an animated, heated rebuttal. The newspapers came to my defense the next day, but I never got the key to the city.

Thankfully, my duties and message before the assembled lords and ladies at Sotheby's were quite different than my fool's errand to Brazil. The program was entirely in English, we were paying our bills, and I was among friends. Promptly at 10:05 p.m. following an introduction by the toastmaster, I began my toast with the proper salutation: "Your Royal Highnesses, Excellencies, my Lords, Ladies, and Gentlemen." When there are several royals in the audience—and there were many this evening—one is permitted to address them in the generic plural. "On behalf of the board of directors, I would like to thank you for honoring us with your presence on this special evening."

I continued: "Two hundred and fifty years ago tomorrow, March

11, 1744, in London, Sotheby's held its first auction. Contrary to published reports, I was not present." (Polite laughter from the assembled lords and ladies.) "But historians tell us that a library of 475 books was sold that day by our founder, Samuel Baker. His nephew, John Sotheby, inherited the firm soon after."

I was nervous but holding my own. "Tonight we celebrate our first 250 years of business. And it is appropriate that we do so here in London, this great city that represents so much of our past accomplishments and so much of our future promise. As an American, I am indeed humbled by the fact that well before there was a United States of America, there was a Sotheby's. In fact, when I learned that my responsibility tonight would be the toast to Sotheby's, a story came to mind that is told about Sir Winston Churchill."

I don't think there is a historic figure I admire more than Winston Churchill, and I incorporate his quotes in my public speaking whenever it makes sense. I hoped this anecdote would effectively communicate the positive aspects of Sotheby's Anglo-American personality.

"In 1942, while reviewing a joint command of British and American troops in North Africa, Sir Winston was warned that the two cultures often clashed most dramatically in, of all places, the officers' mess. The Americans, who religiously drank their whiskey highballs before dinner, forbade alcohol during the meal. The British, on the other hand, allowed no drinking before dinner, but always served claret and burgundy at the table."

I continued: "Faced with the task of toasting the officers that evening, Churchill arrived early and announced, 'Before dinner we Brits will have to defer to the American rules. But at the table, you Yanks must abide by the British regulations.' " (Enthusiastic laughter and applause from the assembled lords and ladies.) "Churchill raised his glass and added, 'I hope this arrangement for the fraternity of Anglo-American relationships will be accepted in good *spirits* by all!' "

The mood in the room changed from rigid formality to genuine celebration. I paid tribute to the memory our former chairman, David Westmorland, and acknowledged the contributions of senior executives: Michael Ainslie, who was just about to step down as chief executive officer; Henry Wyndham, chairman in the U.K.; and Diana Brooks, who was to replace Michael as CEO of Sotheby's in a matter of weeks.

I lifted my glass and concluded with the toast: "We look forward with optimism to our next 250 years. The opportunities are great, as is our commitment. In support of our efforts, I ask you to join me in a toast to Sotheby's. Happy birthday, Sotheby's!"

The room erupted with the words, "Happy birthday, Sotheby's!" What a great evening. Our horizons couldn't have been brighter. At least it seemed that way as the trumpets sounded, the Scots Guards marched into place, and the handsome guests celebrated with champagne in the Colonnade Gallery.

In reality, the company was heading into one of the most difficult and damaging periods in its history. The years ahead were not going to be rosy for me, either. A storm was gathering that would ultimately cripple Sotheby's, rock the art market, and send me to federal prison.

About a year earlier, in February 1993, Michael Ainslie had come to me with a strange proposal. He wanted to buy me out of Sotheby's. He explained that it had become intolerable for him to work with me. Michael felt that I rode him as if he were a junior executive and gave him little real authority to run the organization. Oh, and he had a tentative agreement with First Boston to assist with a management buyout, using my stock as collateral. That's right, Michael was proposing that I allow him to buy Sotheby's using my stock.

I was more surprised than hurt by Michael's proposal. It was beyond naïve of him to think that I would go along with such a deal. But the deterioration of our working relationship did bother me. I liked and trusted Michael. He had been good for Sotheby's, and I respected his leadership abilities. I never kept office space at Sotheby's for myself, and I thought it had been clear to investors, customers, and employees that Michael was running the show. With so many other businesses to look after, I wanted it that way. He was the public voice and face of Sotheby's, and with our public offering, Michael had become a very wealthy man. He deserved every penny.

Many of my closest friends and advisers agreed with Michael that I had been rough on him. I had noticeably changed the way I dealt with him over the previous year or so. I had become impatient with what I interpreted as a deteriorating work ethic. He was constantly traveling, often absent for weeks at a time. Much like Ed Hoffman at Woodies, who had perfected his golf stroke while in my employ, Michael's tennis game was improving by leaps and bounds as he found his way onto the courts of Manhattan, Westchester, and Greenwich at every opportunity.

What I didn't know at the time was that Dede Brooks, who was always nipping at Michael's heels, had put in place an elaborate office intelligence network to alert her to every Ainslie absence. The minute Michael departed from 1334 York Avenue, Dede was informed. After an hour or so—just long enough to let Michael get into his tennis shoes and get onto the court—Dede would call me with an issue requiring immediate attention. I would always ask to get Michael on the line. Of course, Michael was never available. That would set me off and give Dede the chance to be indispensable.

When I informed Michael that I was not interested in facilitating (that is, funding) his "management buyout," he made it clear that he would have to leave the company. When I asked him who would be best to take his place he recommended Dede Brooks without hesitation. She certainly had the talent and drive, although Michael was concerned she might need a bit more maturity and would have to gain respect with colleagues outside the United States.

When I discussed the situation with Jeffrey Miro, my attorney and

Sotheby's board member, he offered an observation I should have taken to heart. "Al," he said, "Dede is a high-risk executive." Max Fisher, who was also on the board, agreed with Jeffrey's prescient warning. No one questioned her smarts, guile, and dedication. But there was something about her character that troubled people. I have to admit that I didn't share or take heed of their concern.

For the most part I had been blessed with honest, ethical partners and associates. In my real estate business, Richard Kughn, followed by Robert Larson, had managed the day-to-day operations of the Taubman Company with impeccable moral standards. Dick and Bob were recognized throughout a rough-and-tumble industry as shining examples of personal integrity and professional competence. I also could trust Bernard Winograd, president of the Taubman Investment Company (the entity whose assets included A&W, Woodward & Lothrop, and Sotheby's), to always take the high road.

In the late 1960s, when we were completing a deal to bring Prudential into the partnership developing Woodland Mall in Grand Rapids, Michigan, I noticed that the good folks at Pru had overpaid us by $400,000. We pointed out the mistake, and it took us several phone calls and meetings to get Pru to understand the error and take their check back. But what's right is right, and we always conducted our business that way.

In 1990, I addressed the Greater Detroit Chamber of Commerce annual conference on Michigan's beautiful Mackinac Island. A focus of the session was ethics. To kick off my keynote remarks with some humor, I told this quick (made-up) story highlighting my relationship with Dick Kughn, who served on the chamber's board of directors:

> The first test of my professional ethics took place very early in my career, when Dick Kughn and I were managing one of our first shopping centers, a project in Flint. In those days, Dick and I visited tenants personally to collect rents.

One day we dropped in on a kind old lady who ran a small family-owned delicatessen. This was my favorite stop for two reasons: the exceptional pastrami and the family's preference for paying the rent in cash.

Dick and I had just handed her a receipt and were on our way out of the store when I looked in her envelope and realized that several crisp $100 bills had stuck together. This struggling deli owner had inadvertently overpaid us by $300.

It was at that moment, as we stepped out the door, that I confronted the first major ethical question of my young career: Do I tell Dick?

The only reason I got away with this (it got a big laugh even at eight in the morning) was the fact that everyone in the audience knew Dick and me to be ethical people. My partners—people like Max Fisher, Les Wexner, Henry Ford II, and Milton Petrie—also were pillars of respectability in their industries and communities. I guess I had developed a blind spot when it came to Dede that even my closest advisers couldn't break through. If the people around you have the courage and comfort level to express honest opinions, you should always listen. And I kick myself whenever I think back on the opportunity I had to avoid disaster. For in this case, trusting the wrong person would turn out to be disastrous—not financially, but personally. My reputation, my family's good name, the company I had spent a lifetime building, my freedom—all would be placed in jeopardy because of my misplaced trust in a key executive.

Dede, who had been heading U.S. operations since 1987, was put in charge of worldwide auction operations in April 1993. That assignment would give her the opportunity to demonstrate her abilities with the intention of giving her Michael's job upon his departure a year later. She did in fact assume the chief executive officer's position—right on schedule—about a month after our 250th anniversary celebration.

Christie's, meanwhile, was going through its own management transition. Christopher Davidge had been promoted to chief executive officer, and Lord Carrington, Christie's highly respected chairman, was to step down in May 1993. Replacing him was Sir Anthony Tennant, who had been a very successful chairman and chief executive at Guiness. Shortly after the announcement of Sir Anthony's Christie's appointment, I met him by chance at a reception at the Royal Academy of Art in London, where we both served on committees. He introduced himself, I wished him the best of luck in his new role, and he asked if I would mind if he called me in the coming weeks to see if we could get together to discuss the auction business. I said sure, and we parted company.

A few weeks later Sir Anthony called my New York office to arrange a meeting. He asked my assistant when I would be in London again, and a breakfast meeting in my London apartment was scheduled for February 3 at 8:30 a.m. Given that Sir Anthony had essentially no experience in the world of art or auctioneering, I was not surprised that he would want to get my perspective on the industry. He was not due to join Christie's for another three months, so I agreed to the meeting with little hesitation. Executives of Sotheby's and Christie's had met together numerous times over the years for very legitimate reasons. For example, every year the two houses coordinate auction schedules in New York and London for the convenience of customers. During Asia Week in New York, Sotheby's and Christie's hold their sales of Asian art in conjunction with art shows, conferences, and cultural exchanges. Committees are formed with representatives from both companies to assure the least possible overlap.

I was also comfortable with our breakfast because I had a clear understanding of and deep respect for our nation's important antitrust and fair trade laws and regulations. The Sherman Antitrust Act was no mystery to me. I had benefited from its enforcement.

Without such government intervention, specialty stores—the life-blood of my shopping centers—would never have been able to compete with department stores for resources.

Back in the 1970s, when I was attending the annual convention of the International Council of Shopping Centers, I stopped in on a session about rents. I was floored to learn that developers were exchanging details of the leases they were signing with national retailers in their malls. When someone asked, "Hey, Al, what's the Gap paying you in your Bay Area centers?" I made quite a scene. I left the meeting, I told everyone about the illegality of their actions, and resigned from the ICSC—prohibiting participation by my company—for more than a decade. I am told this illegal sharing of information never happened again at an ICSC conference, in large measure because of my forceful protest.

I also understood the meaning of "conscious parallelism," a concept in law that explains why it is acceptable for two gas stations on opposite corners of an intersection to offer gasoline at exactly the same price per gallon. Conscious parallelism also allows essentially every residential real estate broker in the country to charge sellers a 6 percent commission to market a home. As long as the parties do not reach an agreement to establish and hold to these prices, the fact that they arrive at the same price is okay with the law. If real estate brokers and gas station owners met to discuss pricing, that would go beyond conscious parallelism and enter the dangerous world of price-fixing.

Traditionally, Sotheby's and Christie's operated with identical commission schedules. That was nothing new. For decades, one house would adjust its rates for buyers and sellers, and the other would follow within weeks to stay competitive—just as the Shell station matches the Mobil station's price for unleaded within a few minutes of an adjustment. And they do it for the same reason: to stay competitive. I knew that it would be both unethical and illegal to discuss pricing with Anthony Tennant or anyone else from Christie's (even though price-fixing was a civil, not criminal offense in the UK). So I welcomed Sir Anthony to my London flat on February 3, 1993, with tea, orange juice, scones, and a clear conscience.

We exchanged pleasantries and discussed the fascinating art market for about an hour. Sir Anthony and I shared a deep respect for the Royal Academy, an expertise in marketing beverages (Guinness for him, A&W root beer for me), and a love for the English countryside. Beyond that, we had little in common. Unlike most of my British friends, Sir Anthony was not an avid sportsman and rarely went on shoots (a polite term for killing birds).

I remember an occasion in the late 1990s when I was walking through an exhibition of Audubon bird prints in Sotheby's New York galleries. Diana Phillips, head of our press office, came around the corner with a group of visiting art journalists. I took advantage of the occasion to opine as to the idiosyncrasies of the various feathered species illustrated on the prints.

One of the reporters asked, "Mr. Taubman, do you collect Audubon prints?"

"No," I replied, "I don't think I have ever purchased an Audubon."

"Then how is it that you have come to know so much about these birds?"

"I've shot every one of them."

Diana abruptly terminated the impromptu interview and skillfully shepherded the journalists away.

When my breakfast discussion with Sir Anthony turned to the spirited and often underhanded competition between our two firms, I took a moment to explain the antitrust laws under which we operate in the United States. Sir Anthony, no stranger to international business, agreed immediately with my insistence that we stay far away from the subject of pricing. That was off the table.

Instead, we agreed that things like bad-mouthing each other in the press, misstating market share, poaching each other's experts, and not following regulations regarding the disclosure of guarantees (a practice we at Sotheby's referred to as "Christie's guarantees") were damaging to both companies and our clients. On a more positive note, we agreed to work together to open the lucrative French market to international auction houses. Because neither Sotheby's nor Christie's was a French company, neither could conduct auctions in France. Political support for this arcane prohibition had been fading, and we had operated an office in Paris for years—a major investment—to demonstrate our commitment to France and keep pushing for change. Christie's had not been as active, and I made it clear to Sir Anthony that we would appreciate their help.

I suppose if Christie's and Sotheby's had formed a trade association for international auction companies, we would have been discussing the same subjects—not in my flat, but in a hotel conference room with PowerPoint presentations and lousy food. Looking back, that certainly would have been smarter for both of us. In the absence of such an organization, Sir Anthony and I met intermittently in London and New York over the next several years. Twelve times in four years, to be exact. Sir Anthony called my office every time to set these up. I never called him. Not once. I must admit that after the first few meetings, I really did not understand why he found the sessions useful. I certainly didn't. Oh, they were pleasant enough, but we had little to talk about (other than the Royal Academy's programs and strategies to overcome political threshold resistance in France).

I would brief Dede Brooks on my discussions with Sir Anthony, and he informed me that he was briefing Christopher Davidge as well. There was no reason to keep our thoughts from them, and with several issues it was important that they follow through on our understandings. For example, our agreement to tone down the public bad-mouthing between the two companies would have been point-less without the CEOs passing our notice of détente on to the troops.

Now, I do not pretend to know what Sir Anthony and Christo-pher Davidge talked about in reference to these meetings. I do know, however, what Dede and I discussed. And never once did we address the subject of pricing or commissions in this context. It hadn't come up in my meetings with Sir Anthony, so there was no reason to re-hash the issue with Dede. Nevertheless, Dede and Davidge at some point (allegedly in 1995, almost two years after my first breakfast with Sir Anthony) decided to go well beyond the legitimate subjects Christie's chairman and I discussed. They proceeded to collude on the setting of new, nonnegotiable commission schedules for sellers at both houses. Dede participated in this illegal act without my knowledge, and certainly without my instructions.

When caught by the authorities in 2000 (and confronted with the fact that her accomplice, Davidge, would testify against her) Brooks would insist—after a number of rejected proffers—that she had been directed by me to break the law. Cleverly, she and Davidge would use the meetings between Sir Anthony and me as proof of my involvement. Certainly, one did not necessarily lead to the other. But the mere existence of the meetings (which I readily admitted to and documented in the voluminous personal diaries and daily office records I turned over to authorities) provided an enticing nexus for the perpetrators looking for an out and the prosecutors looking for a trophy to hang on their wall.

So on the evening of March 10, 1994, as the Scots Guards were marching and the trumpets were sounding in celebration, storm clouds were gathering high above New Bond Street—clouds as dark and ominous as any the company had weathered in its illustrious 250 years. The forecast didn't look too promising for me, either.

~ FIFTEEN ~

Standing Alone

The headline on the front page of the January 29, 2000, *Financial Times* changed a lot of lives around the world: "Christie's Admits Fixing Commissions: Auction House Tells the U.S. Justice Department That It Made Deal with Sotheby's." A photograph of Dede Brooks accompanied the story.

The shocking revelation hit on a Saturday, the day I was celebrating my seventy-sixth birthday in Palm Beach. I heard the news for the first time from my friend art dealer Bill Acquavella, when he and his wife, Donna, arrived at my home that evening for the dinner party Judy had arranged.

"Al, have you heard what's going on? Christie's is admitting to price-fixing with Sotheby's," Bill announced in a low, concerned voice. "It's front-page news in the *Financial Times.*"

I remember being shocked and thinking how irresponsible it was for a respected publication to print such an accusation that was so inaccurate and, for Christie's, self-serving. Impossible. Inconceivable. The U.S. Justice Department had been investigating the art market since 1997, but the consensus was that the probe was going nowhere. And besides, we would never make such a "deal" with Christie's, our archrivals. I know I didn't. And certainly Dede, one of the most competitive people I had ever met, would not have anything to do with such an illegal and destructive arrangement.

My first thought was that those bastards at Christie's, which had been acquired by a private French company in 1998 must have been nailed by the U.S. Justice Department in something sinister and were now throwing false charges at Sotheby's, a publicly held American company, to damage us and negotiate a lesser penalty. I called Dede the next day to hear what she knew about this mess. Instead, I got her husband, who explained that Dede would not be able to speak with me. That's when I really started to be concerned.

Early the next week, I kept a previously arranged appointment with Dede to discuss other matters. When I arrived at our headquarters at 1334 York Avenue, Sotheby's respected in-house general counsel, Don Pillsbury, accompanied me to Dede's conference room, where we could meet in his presence. He thought it best that he sit in on our conversation. Given the circumstances, I agreed. Dede assured us that there was no truth to the charge that Sotheby's had fixed prices with Christie's. She dismissed the *Financial Times* story with subdued confidence. I felt much better hearing her denials.

To break the tension, I held up a copy of the *Financial Times,* pointed to the headline, and said, "I don't think I'd look good in stripes!" (Later in court, testifying under oath, Dede would twist this story to say I had threatened her by saying *she* would look good in stripes. Don Pillsbury testified to the accuracy of my account, but no perjury charges were ever brought against Dede, the government's star witness.) The lighthearted aside, which prompted nervous but audible laughter from Dede and Don, was intended to dismiss the unthinkable outcome of my going to jail. I was relieved to hear Dede's assurances that there was nothing to worry about.

When we met about a week later at my home in Palm Beach, Dede again failed to come clean. She acted as if it were business as usual with Don, Max Fisher, Jeff Miro (on the phone), and me, and left the meeting early to fly to Paris on business. What she didn't tell us was that she had arranged an unauthorized meeting to offer the company for sale to Bernard Arnault, chairman of LVMH Moët Hennessy–Louis Vuitton. Arnault had recently acquired Phillips, a second-tier London-based auction house. Years earlier, Arnault had inquired through his bankers if we were interested in selling Sotheby's. He visited with me in New York and made a verbal offer for my shares. I informed Dede of Arnault's offer, and she encouraged me not to sell, insisting that Sotheby's stock was worth $100 per share. I turned him down, and the discussions never went beyond that preliminary, exploratory stage. Evidently, Dede, acting on her own, felt the time was right to rekindle Arnault's interest—just as the U.S. Justice Department was preparing to charge us with price-fixing!

Over the next few days, it became clearer that Dede had indeed conspired with Christie's CEO, Christopher Davidge, and was prepared to testify that she had done so on my orders. While I knew these charges against me were false, there was mounting pressure on the company for me to step down as chairman. As much as it hurt me to take this step, which I was concerned would be misinterpreted by the board, employees, and the Justice Department as an admission of guilt, I agreed to resign my post. Dede stepped down from her position on the same day, February 21, 2000. Bill Ruprecht, who had worked his way up at Sotheby's through expert, marketing, and senior management positions, stepped in as president and chief executive officer. (He has done a terrific job guiding the company back to strength and profitability.)

At the time, I considered firing everybody on the board (as majority owner, I could technically do that) when they lost confidence in my innocence and me. Who the hell did they think they were? They knew my character. Isn't everybody innocent until proven guilty?

— My wonderful parents, Fannie and Philip —

— A steel crew taking a break on a Federal's Department Store site in Detroit in the mid-1950s. I'm the young guy with the fancy hat seated in the center of the first row. —

— This September 4, 1971 issue of *Business Week* focused on the wave of regional mall development in America. I was lucky enough to be featured on the cover. —

NEW DESIGN'S FACADE brightens surrounding area by night, stands out crisply by day

— I designed this innovative (for the 1960s) fascia treatment for Max Fisher's Speedway 79 gas station chain. We created what was, essentially, a large plastic light box along the front of the service station using just-introduced outdoor fluorescent lighting. Motorists took notice, and Max became my lifelong friend. —

— The closing of our Irvine Ranch acquisition in 1977. Joan Irvine Smith is seated in the center, and Milton Petrie is the first gentleman standing on the left. Next to him is Don Bren, and second from the right is Herbert Allen. —

That's the Great Root Bear on the right. I've been told
there is a striking resemblance.

I designed The Taubman Company's office building in Oak Park, Michigan, which served as our headquarters from 1955 to 1968.

Ed Hoffman of Woodward and Lothrop, Taubman Company president Bob Larson, and me visiting a shopping center in the mid-1980s.

VOL. CCVI NO. 56 ★ ★

Auction Tycoon

To Sotheby's Boss, Selling Art Is Much Like Selling Root Beer

Developer Taubman Employs Old Style in New Field: Aggressiveness and Savvy

Creative or Just Plain Crass?

By MEG COX
Staff Reporter of THE WALL STREET JOURNAL

NEW YORK — A. Alfred Taubman earned a reputation for arrogance as a developer partly because 15 years ago he dared to build shopping malls twice as big as anybody else's, with up to five department stores and amenities like fountains and sculpture. He also dared to charge the highest rents around and to leave stores vacant rather than accept less money or a tenant he didn't want.

Now Mr. Taubman is a billionaire of 60, with multiple homes and jets, and his bulging portfolio includes A & W Restaurants Inc.; a majority interest in the Oakland Invaders, a U.S. Football League team; the department-store chain Woodward & Lothrop; and Sotheby's Holdings Inc., the auction house.

These days he is applying the lessons of his life and trade to 241-year-old Sotheby's, and some say he is turning the venerable London-based auction house into an art department-store and bank. The auction world is still in shock.

"He is the first real businessman to enter the art race," says Martin Ackerman, a New York art-world lawyer and frequent buyer at auctions. "I happen to think he will change the entire nature of the auction business."

A. Alfred Taubman

▬ The *Wall Street Journal* was the first to shorthand—and in the process distort—the intended message of a speech I delivered to the Harvard Business School in 1985. Regrettably, "selling art is like selling root beer" became my slogan and was repeated (and often defended) by journalists around the world despite my best efforts to correct it, or at least place it in context. ▬

▬ This ancient Persian fabric bazaar effectively illustrates the fact that enclosed shopping centers were not invented in the twentieth century. Note the center-court fountain, the skylight, and the corridors housing multiple shops. Sketch in a Starbucks, and you'll have a great-looking contemporay mall. ▬

— Dede Brooks and I posed for this photograph during the renovation of Sotheby's New York office and auction facility on York Avenue. The sparks flying in the background were a sign of things to come. —

THE MONOPOLIES AND MERGERS COMMISSION

A Alfred Taubman and Sotheby Parke Bernet Group PLC

A Report on the Proposed Merger

— I went in front of the Monopolies and Mergers Commission in London in 1983 to share my vision for Sotheby's. They approved and we acquired the venerable auction house soon after. —

Presented to Parliament by the
Secretary of State for Trade and Industry
by Command of Her Majesty
September 1983

LONDON
HER MAJESTY'S STATIONERY OFFICE
£3·30 net

Cmnd. 9046

— The first day of trading for Sotheby's Holdings on the New York Stock Exchange in 1988. With me are Michael Ainslie, then–NYSE president Dick Grasso, and our specialist on the floor, Jack Geary. —

— A Washington, D.C., cartoonist created this shortly after we acquired the Woodward and Lothrop department store company in 1984. Most cartoons bring a smile to my face, even if they are critical of me. I really admire the art form. —

— They pour champagne on you when you win a football championship. With me after the 1983 USFL victory in Denver are Shire Rothbart, Panther coach Jim Stanley, and Max Fisher. —

— My wife Judy and I prepare for a day of shooting at Alnwick Castle in Northumberland. —

Visiting India in 1984 with friends Amy Matouk and Ehab Shafic (left),
recording industry genius Ahmet Ertegun and my wife (center),
and Jerry Zipkin and Mica Ertegun (right).

With my fishing buddies in Iceland: my attorney
Jeffry Miro, Parker Gilbert, Graham Allison, Otto Winckelmann, and
Lord Michael Blakenham.

Relaxing at home in Palm Beach.

My beautiful—but leaky—Richard Meier–designed home in Palm Beach.

My current home in Palm Beach, after major restoration,
which does not leak.

Spending time with my friend Les Wexner at his beautiful home in Aspen, Colorado.

With my daughter Gayle.

Henry Kravis   Alfred Taubman
Jack Geary   George McFadden

Record Score 56 Net
September 21, 1990
Singletree Golf Club
Vail, Colorado

— A great round of golf in Vail. With me are Henry Kravis, Jack Geary, and George McFadden. —

— During my 10-month stay in Rochester, Minnesota, I was inmate 50444-054. I used this card whenever I could to access the delicacies served from the prison's vending machines. I put on my best tough-guy face for the camera, but the experience was terrifying. —

With my sons Robert and William.

Doing my part to thin out the duck population on Long Island.

Karl Lagerfeld took this photograph of my wife Judy and me in 1998. It's one of our favorites.

But underneath my anger I realized this was not just about me. This unthinkable scandal was threatening to bankrupt a 250-year-old company. Starting in January 2000, customers filed civil suits, alleging they had been cheated by the collusion. Investors were fleeing from our stock like rats abandoning a sinking ship. Through no fault of their own, and as the stock fell, Sotheby's employees saw their life savings evaporate. My continued presence on the board was making things worse for everybody.

But stepping down didn't mean giving up. According to *Forbes* and *Fortune,* I was worth hundreds of millions of dollars. But my most precious asset was my good name—the one thing my father had taught me to protect at all costs. I remembered the lengths he went to during the depression to make good on his debts and preserve his reputation.

This was a huge blow, and it was certainly not how I had planned on spending my seventy-sixth year on earth. It was a confusing and difficult time. I was angry and frustrated at Dede Brooks and at the prosecutors, and fearful of what the future might bring me. Developers generally don't look back; we look to the future. It's not that we don't have memories or learn from the past. Rather, when you're involved in a construction project or a leasing campaign, you have to continually move forward, or else you lose time, momentum, and money. Problems have to be faced head-on in a realistic way. That's how I approached my legal difficulties. I had to fight back. And so as I always had done, I set out to find the best professionals I could find.

On the recommendation of Don Pillsbury, we retained the law firm of Davis Polk & Wardwell. Robert Fiske, a former U.S. Attorney and the first Whitewater independent counsel; Scott Muller, a highly respected litigator (Scott served as general counsel to the Central Intelligence Agency for several years after my trial); and Jim Rouhandeh headed the Davis Polk team. They were all exceedingly smart, intensely focused, and seasoned in the complicated world of antitrust prosecution.

This was to be a very messy two-front war. Civil challenges were mounting as a sitting grand jury was determining potential criminal charges. Davis Polk was prepared to lead my defense on both the civil and criminal battlefields. The continuity was very important.

Recognizing that the fight of my life would also be played out in the court of public opinion, Christopher Tennyson, my longtime communications adviser, brought veteran crisis public relations guru John Scanlon on board. With his white beard, red hair, and piercing blue eyes, John looked more like an Irish poet than a tough-as-nails PR guy. But he had earned a reputation for being a first-class advocate for his clients, and he was on a first-name basis with the most important electronic and print journalists in New York. At the first meeting with John in my New York office, at 712 Fifth Avenue, he brought us what he described as very bad news.

"Dede has hired Steven Kaufman, the flipper, and that's not good," said Scanlon.

"What's a flipper?" asked Tennyson.

"An attorney specializing in offering up a superior to make a deal with the prosecutor," Scanlon explained. "Kaufman rarely goes to trial. He has only one play in his playbook, but he runs it very well."

If Dede's strategy hadn't been clear before, it was now. And this time the superior being offered up in exchange for leniency was me.

In one of the many strange and tragic twists in this saga, John Scanlon suffered a fatal heart attack in his Manhattan apartment on May 4, 2001, the morning I was arraigned in U.S. District Court on a single charge of price-fixing. Heading into the eye of the storm, we lost a terrific guy and an important member of our team. Two of John's partners, Lou Colasuonno and Laura Murray, stepped in admirably to assist us.

The civil side of the dispute was relatively cut-and-dried. Dede and Davidge, who had been the CEOs of their respective companies, had admitted their collusion. Both companies, therefore, were guilty as charged. David Boies, the high-profile attorney, represented the "class" of auction house customers that brought suit against Sotheby's and Christie's. He hadn't fared too well in *Bush v. Gore,* but he sure did all right with us. He won a settlement of $256 million from each company for his clients.

Christie's owner, François Pinault, paid all $256 million of his company's portion, and I agreed to contribute $186 million of Sotheby's civil settlements personally. My level of participation was consistent with my majority ownership position. I also was fully aware that without my assistance, the company faced the very real prospect of bankruptcy. These were decisions made out of enlightened self-interest, not charity. Sotheby's represented one of my most significant investments. Abandoning the company and fending for myself would have destroyed a personal asset that, even in the midst of scandal, was worth hundreds of millions of dollars. Besides, all this had happened on my watch. I was committed to the survival of this extraordinary franchise and the preservation of its employees' livelihoods.

David Boies is an interesting guy. I've never met him, but I recently read his book, *Courting Justice.* Chapter 9, "The Auction House Scandal," presents his insightful account of the civil settlement. Boies and I, it turns out, have a lot in common. He, too, suffers from dyslexia. He's a skilled poker player; I do pretty well at bridge. He grew up in Orange County, California, home to the Irvine Ranch. More important, there is probably no one on the planet who studied the evidence in this case with more skill and intensity than Boies. And what was his conclusion? Here's what he told author Christopher Mason in an interview for Mason's meticulously researched book, *The Art of the Steal:*

"There wasn't any real evidence that they fixed prices," Boies noted, referring to Taubman and Tennant, "just that they had a lot of meetings." It was a stunning observation coming from the lawyer who had spent the spring and summer of 2000 poring over documents and taking depositions in an attempt to establish Taubman's guilt.

In other words, after examining all the evidence, Boies concluded that while the two companies' CEOs, Dede Brooks and Christopher Davidge, willingly admitted that they met and agreed to fix prices, there was no evidence that the two companies' chairmen were involved in any way.

One thing David Boies and I do not have in common, however, is our taste in restaurants. In *Courting Justice,* Mr. Boies reveals that when his law firm wrapped up the auction house suits and secured a $26 million fee for four months' work, he celebrated by taking his wife to dinner at Sparks Steak House in Manhattan. I've got nothing against Sparks (John Gotti put the place on the map). But that kind of payday merits a night out at Daniel or, if you want a great steak, Peter Luger in Brooklyn.

Thanks in large measure to David Boies's legal and negotiating acumen, the civil challenges were resolved swiftly (and expensively). But the potential exposure on the criminal side was far more frightening. Over the years, I had dealt with civil litigation many times. It's a hazard and natural byproduct of doing business. There were times I won, and times I lost, and times when settling made economic and business sense. I wasn't happy about paying to settle the civil suits, but I could survive and live with it. This was different. Much different. Criminal prosecution brought with it the prospect of jail time. Was the Justice Department going to pursue criminal charges against me? It was uncertain for all of 2000 and the first quarter of 2001. What was certain, however, was that prosecutors were hard at work making it difficult, if not impossible, for me to defend myself.

From the outset, the deck was stacked against us. In an action that startled even the most seasoned judicial observers, the U.S. Justice Department granted Christie's, a foreign-owned company, and all its employees, including Christopher Davidge, amnesty from prosecution in return for their cooperation in the effort to essentially cripple or destroy Sotheby's and put me in prison.

Now, I understand that the amnesty program has yielded important victories for our country's prosecutors. It's easy to applaud the decision to isolate a mob boss or terrorist by protecting informants from criminal prosecution. But the practice seriously distorts the concept of equal justice. Here's how the writer James B. Stewart, in the October 15, 2001, issue of the *New Yorker,* described the questionable practice in my case:

> Prior to 1993, a price-fixer who wanted amnesty for testifying against a co-conspiring competitor had to take his information to the Justice Department before an investigation was under way. But that year the department began offering amnesty even after an investigation was in progress—to whoever came in the door first and promised that all its employees would confess and cooperate against other conspirators. From a law-enforcement perspective, the program has been a success. Since it began, requests for amnesty, which under the old program had averaged one a year, jumped to more than one a month, and in the last four years the government has reaped fines of $1.7 billion. Many defense lawyers, mindful of the innate American distaste for informers, have argued that such incentives to cooperate are too generous, extravagantly rewarding testimony from people who are criminals and who tailor their testimony to what prosecutors want to hear. But so far none of the cases have generated a public outcry.

Unfortunately, neither would mine, even though Christie's received this "extravagant" treatment without meeting the most fundamental requirements to qualify for the program. First of all, according to the Justice Department's guidelines, the instigator of the price-fixing is ineligible for amnesty. If you started it, forget it. Even to this day, nobody in the world (including the prosecutors, I believe) believes Sotheby's or I started this thing. Not a soul. In Christopher Mason's book, Christie's senior executive François Curiel stated what everybody has always understood to be the truth: "Chris [Davidge] is a chief manipulator with a capital C . . . He did it very, very cleverly." Granting amnesty to the party starting the wrongdoing could lead to all sorts of problems and injustice. But the Justice Department conveniently ignored this disqualification.

According to the rules, you can also forget about amnesty if you fail to come forward in a timely manner with your information. Christie's didn't even come close. The collusion between Dede and Davidge was an open secret at Christie's at the highest levels of the company in London and New York. In 1997, three years *before* Christie's knocked on the door of the Justice Department, Lord Hindlip—the man who succeeded Anthony Tennant as Christie's chairman and who has admitted publicly to knowing in 1995 about the two CEOs getting together to discuss the seller's commissions—provided Davidge with the following handwritten note:

Dear Christopher:

I am writing to assure you that, in the unlikely event that it should happen you are forced to resign your position because of the antitrust hearings in the U.S., Christie's will fully protect your position as per your contract . . .

Testimony in court would reveal that even Christie's new owners were well aware of Davidge's misdeeds long before they decided to "do the right thing." In fact, when confronted with a confession by Davidge, François Pinaut's people didn't head straight to the authorities.

They sweetened Davidge's severance payments in return for his promise of silence! The Justice Department conveniently ignored this disqualification as well.

The power to grant amnesty from prosecution in a criminal trial
is an awesome responsibility. Misused, it has the potential to destroy
our system of justice. That's why Congress granted that power with
carefully crafted rules and guidelines. The antitrust division of the
U.S. Justice Department allowed Christie's to avoid prosecution,
even though the company didn't even come close to qualifying for
the amnesty program.

We are a nation of laws, not men. That bedrock principle was
driven home to me many years ago when I had the honor to attend
the dedication ceremonies for the Damon J. Keith Law Collection of
African American Legal History at Wayne State University in Detroit,
an archive dedicated to the accomplishments of African American
lawyers and judges. Judge Keith, who has served on the U.S. Court of
Appeals for the Sixth Circuit since 1977, is a good friend of mine and
one of the most respected jurists in the country. One of the nation's
first African American federal judges, Damon has written many
landmark decisions and trained many distinguished law clerks.
Michigan's current governor, Jennifer Granholm, started her legal
career clerking for Judge Keith, as did Lani Guinier. Guinier, who is
best known for having been nominated by President Bill Clinton to
be assistant attorney general for civil rights, was the keynote speaker
that evening. She told a story I will never forget.

In the early 1970s, a gang of hateful racists, known as the White
Panthers, bombed the offices of the Central Intelligence Agency in Ann
Arbor, Michigan. The police arrested the bombers, but only after rely-
ing on what turned out to be unauthorized wiretaps. Guinier was
clerking for Judge Keith when the White Panthers' appeal came before
him. As disgusted as he was with the perpetrators and their violent act,
Judge Keith overturned the conviction, rebuking law enforcement

officials who argued that national security gave them the right to ignore established procedures designed to protect the rights of all citizens. Though challenged by President Nixon and Attorney General John Mitchell, Judge Keith's ruling was upheld by the U.S. Supreme Court. Guinier explained that the young law clerks, many of them African Americans, were at first upset when Judge Keith arrived at his difficult decision. But as he explained to them the overriding importance of the Constitution and the rule of law, they learned a very important lesson—a lesson they carried with them into their distinguished legal careers. For that higher wisdom, they loved and respected Damon even more than they had before.

I can tell you that I love Damon, too. He testified at my trial as a character witness. It was the first time in his life he had testified in court. Many people were displeased with the willingness of a sitting judge to speak in my defense. Thankfully, he ignored their protests and endured what I thought were disrespectful, smart-ass remarks by the prosecution and dismissive treatment by the judge at my trial. The world and certainly the Justice Department would be better off with more Damon Keiths.

There was more to do to assure my conviction. The Justice Department was preparing to allege that Anthony Tennant and I decided to fix prices during our second meeting, on April 30, 1993. There were only two people in the room that morning—Anthony Tennant and me. What did Sir Anthony have to say about this? The jurors would never know. The Justice Department indicted Tennant, a British citizen, in the United States. He was the only Christie's employee *not* to receive amnesty. And this act assured he would be unavailable to shed light on the matter. Understanding that the charge of price-fixing in the U.K. carries only civil penalties, Sir Anthony would have been a fool to travel to the U.S. for a trial on criminal charges. I didn't blame him for that. But I did resent the prosecutors' cynical strategy. Tennant would have been a key witness in my defense. He was the only other person in the room with firsthand knowledge to support or refute the charges against me. And he was prevented from testifying.

What would Sir Anthony have said if called to the witness stand? Christopher Mason interviewed Sir Anthony for his book:

> Tennant firmly denied that he told Davidge to fix prices with Dede Brooks. "The proposition that as chairman I had given Davidge instructions is almost laughable. Davidge did whatever he wanted to and didn't inform me. I didn't see him very often," he added.
>
> A crime had clearly been committed by Davidge and Brooks, Tennant said, but he and Taubman had nothing to do with it. "Why the hell would I want that sort of thing? And why would Al?" Having admitted their own culpability, Tennant observed, Brooks and Davidge "had transparently obvious reasons for putting the finger on Al and me."

There was an even more important reason for the prosecution to keep Tennant off the stand. In the thousands of pages of documents Davidge had provided the Justice Department, my name never came up. Not once. The center of the government's case against me was a "memo" written in Sir Anthony's hand that purportedly reflected our discussion on April 30, 1993. The memo, which was really a bunch of notes, never mentioned my name. But Davidge was prepared to testify that Tennant had given him his notes and told him they represented *my* thoughts at the meeting. That's called hearsay. But the notes ultimately would be admitted into evidence, and they would prove very damaging. What would Sir Anthony have said regarding the legitimacy of the prosecution's key document? Again, Mason's interview answers that crucial question:

> It never was a memo, he said. "I don't think I've ever sent a memorandum without signing it or addressing it to someone. I don't think

anyone does. And there's no record of any offer, or any acceptance of an agreement, in that thing. They made it seem to be a very sinister document. And that suited everybody except poor Al, who didn't know what the hell it was about, I imagine.

Instead, the "memo" was merely three pieces of paper on which Tennant had jotted down a series of notes over several days, weeks or months—an assertion that appeared to square with the discovery by Taubman's lawyers that the two different kinds of paper had been used: one sheet had faint blue lines, and the other two, faint gray lines. The various unrelated paragraphs, Tennant said, "were all written at different times."

What's more, Tennant told Mason that much of the material in the memo reflected information actually given to him by Christopher Davidge, the government's key witness! How did Davidge get the memo? "He [Tennant] had no recollection of ever showing, or giving, them to him. According to Tennant, Davidge was the only person who knew the secret combination number to the door to the chairman's private office." Ultimately, the jury members would be misled as to the content and purpose of the memo, and they would never be told that the prosecution's protected witness had the notes!

Now, Tennant may or may not have been unable to destroy the prosecution's case if he had been present in the court. But as Mason concludes: "Whether true or not, Tennant's articulate reflections could at the very least have created substantial reasonable doubt in the minds of the jury members, which could have resulted in an acquittal for the aging tycoon." The aging tycoon, of course, is yours truly.

I was increasingly frustrated by the efforts of my own government to stack the deck against me *before* trial, so I turned to my (very expensive) lawyers for help. What could I do to establish my innocence?

They came up with an intriguing but high-risk suggestion: a poly-graph examination. A lie detector test! I jumped at the opportunity even after hearing the reason my attorneys considered it high risk. In most instances, the results—good or bad—would not be accepted as evidence at trial. And in just about every case, the results, if bad, would find their way to the prosecutors and probably be leaked to the press.

Nevertheless, I thought it was important to give my attorneys proof that I was telling them the truth. I thought they would work harder for me with that assurance. And I wanted something I could share with my former colleagues on the board at Sotheby's. Their trust was very important to me.

So on October 3, 2000, I flew to Virginia to put my fate in the hands of Paul K. Minor, the highly respected former head of the FBI's poly-graph division. For more than an hour I was wired up to Minor's ma-chine—the test reminded me of the many electrocardiograms I have taken in my life—and asked a series of questions designed to get to the truth. The central questions were very specific:

- Did you and Tennant have an agreement regarding amounts to be charged to buyers or sellers?
- Did you tell Dede Brooks to try to reach an agreement with Davidge regarding amounts to be charged to buyers or sellers?
- Did Dede Brooks ever tell you that she had reached an agreement with Davidge about amounts to be charged to buyers or sellers?

I answered no to all three. Minor's findings: absolutely no decep-tion. I was telling the truth. We shared the results with the Justice Department and with Don Pillsbury, who passed copies of the official report along to the Sotheby's board. Predictably, the prosecutors ignored the information. But I felt good about having something, anything, to help support my case with people close and important to me. It's a terrible feeling to see your credibility eroded by powerful forces you can't control. To this day, I am the only individual associated with this scandal who has submitted to a lie detector test. Imagine if the Justice Department introduced a new requirement for anyone seeking amnesty from the Justice Department: no polygraph test, no amnesty. I can only imagine how such a common-sense regulation would have changed the course of this prosecution and my life. On May 2, 2001, I was charged with a single count of price-fixing. As we suspected, so was Anthony Tennant, a move that would keep his crucial testimony from getting in the way of the prosecution's hardwired case. I pleaded not guilty.

— SIXTEEN —

United States of America v. A. Alfred Taubman

On November 8, 2001, the trial in the matter of *United States of America v. A. Alfred Taubman* got under way in United States District Court, Southern District of New York.

The testimony would be heard in the first-floor "ceremonial courtroom" of the federal courthouse, just blocks from the World Trade Center site, scene of the devastating 9/11 terrorist attacks only one month earlier. In fact, the trial had been delayed because of the difficult recovery efforts in lower Manhattan. The weather was unusually warm for November, with temperatures in the eighties. The indescribable odor still wafting from Ground Zero made its way into the halls of the venerable courthouse.

The presence of heavily armed security forces and defensive concrete barriers around the courthouse added to what for me was an already terrifying experience. Everyone entering the building had to pass through a single security checkpoint thirty or forty yards from the massive courthouse steps. This created the ideal opportunity for the press and paparazzi to ambush me every morning. It was fascinating (and a bit frightening) to witness the aggressive strategies and pack mentality of these folks. What a way to make a living. Several would actually bump or trip me as others snapped what would be particularly unflattering shots. I did get in a few well-placed blows. One particularly obnoxious CNN cameraman almost lost his equipment as I scored a direct hit with my umbrella!

Inside, the atmosphere was more theatrical. Luminaries such as author Dominick Dunne and actress Sigourney Weaver attended regularly. Weaver was observing the action in preparation for a proposed HBO movie on the scandal and the trial. She was to play the role of Dede Brooks. (There were rumors that my part would be portrayed by Brad Pitt, but we could never confirm them.) Behind the phalanx of high-powered attorneys sat rows of international reporters, many from the art world press, who gave the audience a certain bohemian character. The jury would often turn away from the day's testimony to gaze at the visitors.

My daughter, Gayle, who has a home in New York City, accompanied me to court every day. She was a source of strength for me as I faced this unpredictable ordeal. Robert and William were minding the store back in Michigan at the Taubman Company, and my wife, Judy, made things as comfortable and normal as possible in our Midtown apartment. I asked her to stay at home, and the lawyers agreed. If she had been in the courtroom with me every day, we both would have relived every moment into the evening. I needed that break from the pressure and frustration, and she was kind to understand.

Although I had been in business for more than fifty years, I had spent very little time in courtrooms. The only time I had ever taken the witness stand was in the 1980s. I was suing architect Richard Meier, who had designed my home in Palm Beach. It was a terrific house, but it leaked whenever it rained beyond a drizzle. Richard had failed to remedy the situation, so I paid to make the necessary repairs and design changes myself. When he refused to reimburse me, I went to court to recover around $800,000 from his insurance company.

The trial attracted plenty of media attention (reporters love it when two rich and/or famous people go after each other in public). Actually, Richard and I got along very well, even in court. When I was called to testify—following a number of roofers, architects, and insurance adjusters—Richard's attorney spent the better part of a morning reviewing all my earthly possessions. To establish my financial position for the jury (and the fact that I certainly didn't need the $800,000), he would read the name of a partnership, the title of a painting, the location of a property. In response to each I was permitted only a one-word answer to the question, "Mr. Taubman, do you own this?" Yes or no. And the judge strictly enforced my brevity.

At the end of this recitation, the attorney turned to the jury and in his most dramatic voice directed one last question to me: "Now, Mr. Taubman, would you agree that you are one very wealthy man?"

"Yes," I answered. "I'm a wealthy man with a leaky house!"

The jury burst out in laughter and awarded me the money. Even Richard Meier congratulated me on my testimony.

But this was different. Very different. *United States v. A. Alfred Taubman!* I don't think the full impact of what I was facing hit me until the husky female clerk entered the courtroom and announced, "The United States of America versus A. Alfred Taubman." The country I loved—the best, most powerful nation on earth—was asking a jury of my peers to send me to prison. The country I fought for in World War II was using every legal weapon in its arsenal to take my freedom for something others had done. What an empty, helpless feeling.

Judge George B. Daniels presided over the trial. We didn't know much about him. He had served as legal counsel to New York mayor David Dinkins and had joined the federal bench in April 2000. Judge Daniels had attended Yale University at the same time Dede Brooks was matriculating there, but no one was suggesting that they had known each other.

Judge Daniels denied our motions time and again. For example, he ruled that Christopher Davidge could participate in the trial, even though the former Christie's CEO was being directly compensated (around $8 million) by his former employer to testify against me. Imagine the potential for abuse when witnesses are permitted to be paid for specific testimony.

Once the trial got going, things went from bad to worse. Critical exculpatory testimony by my New York assistant, Melinda Marcuse, was not allowed. A key document we were planning to use in our defense—proving that Christie's had reached out to Sotheby's deputy chairman, Lord Camoys, not me, around the time of the collusion—was not permitted to be entered into evidence. Judge Daniels was concerned the facts would be "confusing" to the jury. These rulings were devastating. In our appeal, we stated it this way:

> The record thus demonstrates that admitting the evidence would have caused no prejudice or confusion, while excluding it caused both. Once again, the court erred on the side of exclusion: the government took improper advantage of the error; and Taubman was prevented from putting on his case.

Davidge (whom I had never met) and Dede took a novel approach to their testimony. They readily admitted to being liars. One particularly memorable exchange between Scott Muller and Christopher Davidge went like this:

MULLER: You remember lying through your teeth, right?
DAVIDGE: I wouldn't say it was through my teeth, but I did lie.

It was hard to determine if the jury would believe anything from these witnesses. We used my flight logs and Brooks's itinerary to establish that her account of the date and time at which I allegedly told her to break the law was impossible. When we confronted her, she deftly backed off her recollections. When she testified that I had given her a handwritten summation of my April 30 meeting with Sir Anthony (anyone who works with me knows I never take notes or pass along handwritten memos), she reported that she had not kept the note. We asked for schedules documenting the times of her meetings with Christopher Davidge, because we strongly suspected that she and Davidge had begun meeting well before I ever met Sir Anthony Tennant. But she informed the court that she always destroyed her diaries at the end of each calendar year.

Would the jury find this level of obfuscation credible? I didn't want to take any chances. I wanted to take the stand, look these people in the eye, and profess my innocence. If they were going to side with me, I had to tell them what Sir Anthony (who was still a mystery to them) and I discussed in our breakfast meetings. I had to address the ridiculous assertion that I would tell Dede Brooks, who rarely followed anyone's orders, to go break the law. The jury members had given up weeks of their busy lives to consider my case. I owed them as much time as they needed to get to know me better.

An enormous amount of threshold resistance existed between the jury members and me. I could feel it every day during the four-week trial. I saw it in their eyes as they glared at me from the jury box. They didn't like me or relate to me. They mistrusted everything about the auction business. The prosecutors had done an excellent job of making the selling of art sound downright sinful. They just wanted to get back to their lives. I was not a legal expert, but I was pretty good at sizing up people and assessing threshold resistance. There was plenty of work to do before these folks could ever rule in my favor.

That was my read. My attorneys didn't agree. When it came time to decide if I would testify, my legal team felt that we had established reasonable doubt in the minds of the jurors. And jurors—at least in theory—must acquit if the prosecutor fails to establish guilt beyond a reasonable doubt. As Bob Fiske declared in his closing argument, "I

tell you, Dede Brooks is a walking reasonable doubt." Our "jury expert" (whom the jurors referred to as "Eagle Eye" because she stared
at them throughout the trial) was sure they liked me and mistrusted
Dede and Davidge. Subjecting myself to what could be days of government cross-examination would risk all that. And besides, I didn't
remember every detail of every meeting with Sir Anthony. Each "I
don't remember" would be held against me.

Ultimately, it was my decision to make. I didn't get a wink of sleep
that night. In the morning, I ignored every instinct in my body and
went with my legal team's recommendation. They were the experts.
I put my life in their hands and did not take the stand.

In final arguments, prosecutor John Greene had one more surprise up his sleeve. He offered the jury a quote from the eighteenth-
century economist Adam Smith (Bob Fiske forcefully pointed out to
Judge Daniels that the economist had not testified in this trial). In his
landmark work, *An Inquiry into the Nature and Causes of the Wealth of Nations,*
Smith wrote:

> People in the same trade seldom meet together even for merriment
> and diversion, but the conversation ends in a conspiracy against the
> public or in some contrivance to raise prices.

Despite our aggressive objections to this last-minute hearsay
from what John Greene had identified as "a famous economist,"
Judge Daniels allowed the off-the-wall, prejudicial quote to be read
to the jury. Greene failed to explain that Smith published this base-
less assertion way back in 1776 (the guy was a contemporary of Ben
Franklin, not Ben Stein) and the otherwise diligent prosecutor neglected to enter Smith's next sentence into the record,:

> It is impossible indeed to prevent such meetings, by any law which ei-
> ther could be executed, or would be consistent with liberty and justice.

So even Adam Smith himself had warned future prosecutors in his very next sentence against embracing his observation out of context. In our appeal, we argued, "the Smith quotation is wholly inconsistent with, and therefore effectively misstates, the governing principles of antitrust law . . . the law is that neither meetings between competitors nor the exchange of information between them is per se, or even presumptively, unlawful." The appeals court agreed with us and chastised Greene for this indiscretion, stating, "We now consider the Government to be on notice that future uses of a quotation such as the one used in this case might prove fatal to its case." Shame on you. Just don't do it again.

We also lost on our effort to have Judge Daniels explain in his instructions to the jury that meetings between competitors are not necessarily illegal. Here's the requested instruction that was never read to the jurors:

> Evidence of meetings, telephone calls, or other contacts between Mr. Taubman and Anthony Tennant and between Mr. Taubman and Diana Brooks does not by itself prove that Mr. Taubman was a participant in a conspiracy or that he had the required knowledge and intent. Competitors may have legitimate and lawful reasons to have contacts with each other or to exchange information or statements of intention. Thus you may not infer that Mr. Taubman knowingly and intentionally joined the conspiracy solely from the fact that he had meetings or other contacts with Christie's or participated in exchanges of information with Tennant.
>
> Similarly, evidence that competitors exchanged price or commercial information or stated their intentions concerning prices or commercial terms which they have charged or the prices or commercial terms which they intend to charge does not by itself prove that someone knowingly joined a conspiracy, even if the exchange of information was done by agreement. It is not unlawful for competitors

to meet and give, obtain or exchange information on independently derived prices. Similarly, it is not unlawful for competitors to meet and discuss proposed industry laws and regulations, compliance with existing laws and regulations, issues relating to business ethics and standards, and other matters of common concern to the industry.

That's an accurate statement of the law. The government's lawyers had no objection to this guidance being added to Judge Daniel's instructions. The judge, however, stated that the jurors — the fork lift operator, the postal worker, the deli owner—would have to be "out to lunch" to not understand these finer points of antitrust law already. Consequently, they never heard these critical instructions before they began to deliberate on December 4.

The deliberations weren't particularly deliberate. From the holding room we had in the back of the court, we could hear the jurors talking; not every word, but when there were loud exchanges, we could make out muffled sounds. Just before the jury returned their verdict—after about ten hours of deliberations over two days—we heard cheers and applause from the jury room. I knew that couldn't be good.

As I stood in court waiting for the foreman to read the jury's verdict, I was numb. I could not believe my country was doing this to me. Despite my attorneys' optimism and assurances, I knew we had not been able to make our case. "Guilty."

While the outcome was not a surprise, hearing that word took the breath out of me. I turned to see the look of sadness and defeat on the face of my daughter, Gayle. There was all sorts of commotion in the courtroom, but all I could see was Gayle's face and the tears in her eyes.

Outside the courthouse, media gathered to report the outcome of the trial and interview the jurors, who were more than happy to get their fifteen seconds of fame on CNN. One juror, however, was reluctant to chat. Lydell Durant had held out as the one remaining "not guilty" vote until the bitter end. Crusty *New York Post* columnist Steve Dunleavy (I find him refreshingly irreverent) spotted Mr. Durant's troubled expression and pulled him around the corner for an exclusive conversation. The headline on Dunleavy's column the next day read: "In My Heart, I Don't Believe He Is Guilty." The troubled juror told Dunleavy, "I think it was the wrong verdict. I didn't sleep last night; I can't tell you what was going through my mind in the jury room, but deep down, I feel Mr. Taubman was not guilty, and I am very sad."

Not until Christopher Mason's book was published more than a year later would we find out what was going on in Mr. Durant's mind in the jury room: He was being "coerced" by the other jurors. Juror Glenn Forrester proudly admitted to Mason in an interview: "We *did* coerce him."

As an American, I'm sorry Lydell Durant had to face that kind of treatment by his fellow citizens. As the guy who ended up in jail because of this violation of one of our most sacred civic responsibilities, I'm even more sorry.

Along with my lawyers and family, we drove uptown to my office at 712 Fifth Avenue. Sentencing was set for April 22. We all gathered in the conference room to consider an appeal and try to make sense out of what just happened. All I wanted to do was apologize to my wife, children, and grandchildren. I was leaving them with a terrible burden. Our name—their name—had been damaged forever. My father never did such a thing to me. "I'm sorry for what I've done to you."

As one, they insisted that they couldn't be more proud of me, our name, and how I had fought the good fight. They found hope in the appeals process and professed faith and trust in our judicial system to right this wrong. I wish I could have been as optimistic. Our criminal justice system is the best in the world. I still believe that. But it didn't work for me.

That afternoon I made many difficult phone calls. I wanted to resign immediately from the corporate boards I sat on and the civic organizations I helped lead. The last thing I wanted to do was to put them in an awkward position. All accepted my resignations, reluctantly and graciously, and most expressed hope that my appeal would be successful and I would be able to rejoin them. Stepping away from my role as chairman of the Taubman Company after more than fifty years was painful. It was in good hands with my son Robert at the helm. But to know that I would no longer be a part of the company I founded with my father—the company that had accomplished so much in communities across the country—was especially hard for me.

At the sentencing hearing a few months later, I was asked by Judge Daniels if I had anything to say. I had plenty to say, but there was no way I could say it to him. My lawyers had explained that anything short of a confession of guilt and an expression of remorse would be counterproductive. Here's the catch-22: to admit guilt after defending my innocence all these months just to lessen the chances of jail time would subject me to charges of perjury.

Hey, I wasn't guilty. And I wasn't about to beg for mercy. Sure, I was sorry this all happened. Sorry I had ever met with Sir Anthony Tennant. Sorry I hadn't listened to my closest partners when they warned me about Dede Brooks. Sorry Judge Daniels and the Justice Department had made it impossible for me to get a fair trial. Sorry that the talented, hard-working people at Sotheby's had to suffer.

The probation officer's report to the judge recommended no jail time, just probation and a fine. So I respectfully declined Judge Daniel's kind offer and kept my thoughts to myself.

My wife, Judy, was with me and prepared for the worst. Chronicling that day in court for *Vanity Fair,* Dominick Dunne wrote:

> Then the glamorous Judy Taubman walked into the courtroom from
> a door to the left of the judge's bench, which jurors had used during

the trial. It was her first appearance in the courtroom. She was perfectly dressed in beige, looking both stylish and understated. All eyes were on the international social figure. She looked straight ahead, making eye contact with no one . . . Then Alfred Taubman entered the courtroom from the same door. He is still massive, and wonderfully tailored, but there was a look of defeat on his face that I had not seen earlier. Before he took his seat, he went to the first row and walked down the line of his family members. Everyone rose and kissed him. When he got to Judy, she looked at him with a loving smile and stood up and kissed him on the lips. Her moment had come, and she rose to it.

Ignoring the probation officer's recommendation, which is rare in criminal cases, Judge Daniels sentenced me to one year in prison. Upon hearing the sentence, Bob Fiske jumped up and requested that it be revised upward to a year and a day. Boy, I thought, Fiske should be on my side! As it turned out, the extra day qualified me for time-off consideration, making my time in prison more like ten and a half months. Judge Daniels accepted our motion.

A week after my sentencing, Judge Daniels let Dede Brooks off with absolutely no jail time. Her punishment: six months' house arrest in her midtown apartment. The "flipper" had added another notch to his belt.

It was no surprise to me when our appeal to the United States Court of Appeals for the Second Circuit went nowhere. "Al, courts don't like to overturn jury decisions, no matter how flawed," an attorney friend explained to me. But we tried. We even added Seth Waxman, former solicitor general of the United States, to our legal team. The three-judge panel hearing our appeal found in July 2002 that all sorts of errors had been committed during the trial—all of it "harmless." My focus now was on preparing to go to prison and somehow make the best of it.

A final thought about the trial. Much has been said and written in criticism of my attorneys' strategy and presentation. At times I must admit I felt they were far too gentlemanly, businesslike, and cautious to connect with the jury. For example, Rosa Parks, the late, courageous civil rights pioneer, was agreeable to appearing on my behalf as a character witness at trial. I had become part of Rosa Parks's life through a terrible incident in Detroit, where she lived from 1957 to her death in 2005. In 1994, this icon of the civil rights movement was attacked and robbed in her home. Judge Damon Keith called me the next day to see if we could arrange for safer living arrangements. Max Fisher and I immediately got her an apartment in our Riverfront Apartments and made sure she never had to worry about rent or robbery ever again. It was an honor to get to know this heroic, graceful woman and to contribute in a small way to her safety and comfort for the last eleven years of her life. Would her presence in court have made a difference? We'll never know. My legal team considered her participation "over the top." Looking back, I think I could have used the help.

I didn't like Judge Daniels. But my anger against him didn't really develop until years after the trial when I read a front-page story in the December 6, 2004, issue of the *New York Times*. The headline read: "Judge's Decisions Draw Notice for Being Conspicuously Late." Here are the lead paragraphs of the story by reporter Benjamin Weiser:

> They are kept in federal courthouses across the United States, although, understandably, they are not prominently displayed: lists of cases that have dragged on for months or even years, often because a judge has failed to make a ruling.
>
> But there is one unchallenged king of the delayed decisions: Judge George B. Daniels of Federal District Court in Manhattan, who, the latest statistics show, had 289 motions in civil cases pending for more than six months, the highest total of any federal judge in the nation.

Judge Daniels was prompt in my case. Unfair, I felt, but punctual. There was plenty of press attention to spur things along. But in cases dealing with everyday folks out of the media spotlight, his inattention has been outrageous:

> There was the woman in Queens who had to fend off creditors while she waited more than three years for the judge to decide that she was entitled to her late husband's pension benefits. And there was the prisoner with H.I.V. who filed a petition challenging his state court conviction. By the time Judge Daniels got around to issuing the order—three years later—the prisoner had died.

In comparison to how others have fared in front of Judge Daniels, I'm a lucky guy!

— SEVENTEEN —

50444-054

On August 1, 2002, I was supposed to report to the Federal Medical Center in Rochester, Minnesota. That's a fancy name for a federal prison where inmates with medical conditions are held for a time before returning them to traditional facilities. The center is loosely affiliated with the nearby Mayo Clinic. At seventy-eight years old, I wasn't in the best of health, having suffered several minor strokes and battled a number of lesser ailments. As rough as they had been with me in court, the Feds didn't want me to die in jail.

A few days before my last day of freedom, Chris Tennyson called to alert me to a strange media request.

"Mr. Taubman, you're not going to believe this. Several news magazines and wire services are asking what time you plan to arrive in Rochester. They want to make sure they get great photos of you checking into prison."

What a way to make a living.

"Obviously, we don't want to give them anything. Should we find out if there's a back door," asked Chris, "or maybe you show up before the sun comes up?"

I appreciated Chris's concern. No way did I want to be on the cover of *Business Week,* entering prison. But I had a better idea.

"I'll check in a day early."

There was silence on the line. I think Tennyson had thought I'd gone crazy. After all, who would ever want to push up the date of his incarceration? After what seemed like an eternity, Chris promised to check to see if such an arrangement was possible.

The warden was happy to accommodate my new arrival date. So, on the morning of July 31, I thanked my household staff and asked them to hold down the fort, kissed my wife good-bye and boarded my Gulfstream IV for the less-than-one-hour flight from Pontiac to Rochester—a day earlier than anyone in the media expected (boy, were they disappointed). Accompanying me were my son Bobby and my attorney, Jeff Miro.

Most people have to think a moment before they can point to the worst day or moment of their lives. Not me. Walking through the gates of the prison I could not leave for the better part of a year was hands down the most sickening experience of my life. I wasn't so much frightened as I was numb. I felt mentally prepared, reaching back to my years in the army during World War II for inner strength. At least no one in the Federal Medical Center was going to shoot at me or drop bombs in my direction. If this was what my government wanted me to do, I would do it, just as I had done back in 1942. I lived through that; I can live through this. That was my attitude going in.

I entered a room in the guardhouse. They took everything I had away from me, including the clothes I was wearing, and put my possessions in a box and sent them home. As I stood there naked, a guard inspected every body cavity. I was given recycled army attire to wear—no shoes, socks, or belt—and led to another room inside the compound, beyond the two forty-foot fences, which were topped with barbed wire. These towering barriers were separated by an asphalt drive. A security vehicle constantly patrolled between the fences, just in case some unlucky inmate made it past the inner fence.

I was directed to change into another outfit of army surplus garb. This time they did allow me to wear ill-fitting slippers. In still another building, I was taken to a downstairs room where I was photographed, issued the number 50444-054, and outfitted in a better-fitting shirt and trousers, along with underwear, socks, and shoes.

Then I was taken to a room with seven beds. This is where I would sleep, I was told, during my three to six days of orientation. With me were two other recent arrivals. One was from Hawaii. The other was a big, strong thirty-six-year-old African American named Ben. He was from Cleveland, and right away we got along. Ben, who had already been in the prison system for eleven years, was serving a twenty-year sentence for a drug-related conviction. He was intelligent, had a good sense of humor, and from our first day together in Rochester he became my advisor and protector, which I appreciated very much.

After the orientation period, I was assigned to my permanent room. It really wasn't what you think of as a cell. It was more like a hospital room, with a standard door. My roommate was a thirty-nine-year-old Mexican-born fellow from California. He was serving the last three years of a fifteen-year sentence for dealing drugs. We got along fine. In fact, he repeatedly asked me to adopt him. His plan for when he got out was to become a member of the Taubman family. This was a complicated matter, I explained to him. It would require a thorough review by my children, who would have to decide if they wanted him as their brother, and by my estate trustees. We discussed his proposal many times—he would wake me up in the middle of the night to repeat the merits of his plan—but we never closed the deal. (I still get mail from him, though. He ends his letters: "Best to my family and to stepmom Judy.")

One thing you learn right away as you interact with the other inmates is to never show any signs of disrespect. An inadvertent bump in the lunch line may be interpreted as a major personal affront. Pride is the only thing inmates have left to protect—everything else has been taken away. The guards regard you as a number, not a person. Your schedule is determined, your every move directed. Since my release, many friends have asked me if the prison administration wanted me to teach a course on real estate or business. Believe me, such enrichment and interaction are not high priorities. I was never asked to do anything other than show up for roll calls and follow directions.

Essentially, the prison is a human warehouse, plain and simple. Prison officials are in the human warehousing business, storing people away for a period of time. From my experience, there is nothing correctional about the environment of a federal prison. Not even close.

The warden was a good man, and he did the best job he could within the system. He wasn't given a lot to work with. Even though Rochester was an all-male facility, the prison's medical director was a gynecologist! And the budget for food, I learned, was $2.52 per day for each inmate. Thank goodness we had a clever food administrator, who did wonders with the crap he was given (the inmates were the cooks). Almost every can of corn, peas, and soup he worked with had an expired "must be eaten by" date on the label. If something should have been consumed by July, we were eating it in January. It really was like being back in the service!

Everything had strict limits, and you had to understand the boundaries to get along. For instance, there was a point system that determined the number of visitors an inmate could have. We got fifteen points per month. Each weekday visit counted as one point. Visits on weekends or holidays counted as two. My son Bobby set up an elaborate schedule of visits by my friends and family (each of whom had to be prescreened and approved by the Bureau of Prisons), making efficient use of the allotted points.

Phone time was also carefully supervised. Every conversation was recorded, and it was a no-no to discuss business. The people you called also had to be preapproved by prison officials, and you were not permitted to transfer a call or patch in another party. That's the only rule I ran afoul of while in the big house. While talking with my assistant Melinda Marcuse one day, I learned that my dear friend Max Fisher, who was ninety-three at the time, had been rushed to a hospital in Palm Beach. I had to talk with him to make sure he was all right.

"Melinda, transfer me to the hospital. I have to talk with Max."

"I can't do that, Mr. Taubman."

"I have to talk with Max!"

"One moment, sir."

That's what I heard played back to me at my disciplinary hearing the next day. My counselor, who was a decent guy, made sure I had an opportunity to tell my side of the story. I pleaded my case but lost my phone rights for seven days. Believe me, that was a major punishment. When you lose your freedom, every contact with the outside world is precious.

On that score, I was truly blessed. My wife, children, their spouses, my grandchildren, and friends made regular pilgrimages to Rochester. They came with love, conversation, quarters for the vending machines, news of the wonderful world outside the walls, and hope. My granddaughter Ghislaine took her first steps during one of these precious visits. When my wife arrived one day with the medical device I need to breathe at night (I was suffering from sleep apnea), she was told that the only way they could accept it was through the mail. On her way back to the plane that evening she dropped the machine off at a UPS store in Rochester and sent it overnight back to the prison. It eventually got to me, and I slept much better.

Plenty of mail arrived daily. The personal notes were uplifting. I received correspondence from friends, customers, employees of my companies, and folks I had never met from all over the world. Many wrote several times. Tom Monaghan, founder of Domino's Pizza and former owner of the Detroit Tigers, whom I hadn't heard from in years, took the time to check in with me on a regular basis with his best wishes and prayers. Nancy Kissinger was kind enough to send me pictures of her new puppy. The newspapers and magazines also helped keep me sane. It really is a different experience reading *Art & Auction* or *Vanity Fair* in a federal penitentiary.

Not everyone in the Federal Medical Center was so lucky. Close to 90 percent of the men I met—most were African Americans or Latinos—were serving time for nonviolent drug-related offenses. Thanks to mandatory sentencing guidelines, they were taken away from their families and communities for outrageous lengths of time—many for more than twenty years. In almost every case, their wives had divorced them, their children had lost touch, and their communities had forgotten them. They received no mail, welcomed no visitors, and had little hope.

My worst day in Rochester—other than the day I walked into that guardhouse—came in December when Attorney General John Ashcroft sent out a directive limiting the discretionary authority of wardens and other law enforcement officers. Concerned that criminals were getting off too lightly, Ashcroft mandated that all prisoners must serve at least 90 percent of their sentences. Until that point, all indications were that I was going home before my birthday at the end of January. Ashcroft added at least five and a half months to my stay.

The most distressing thing to happen in this period had nothing to do with prison. On November 13, 2002, just a few months into my stay in Rochester, the Simon Property Group launched a hostile takeover attempt against Taubman Centers, Inc. Political scientists note that democratic nations rarely attack other nations. In the business world, it used to be true that family businesses didn't attack other family businesses. So much for history. Simon had locked itself into an acquire-or-die growth strategy and saw us as easy prey. David Simon, son of company founder Melvin Simon, told my son Bobby that the action was intended to strike at us while we were most vulnerable. They were betting that the embarrassment of my conviction would weaken the company's resolve to insist on fair value for its shares. Keep in mind that Mel and his brother Herb Simon had been friends of mine—at least I thought they were—for decades. In fact, just a few weeks before Simon Property Group's attack, I received a very warm letter from Mel.

He let me know that he was in a "funk" about my jail sentence and expressed how badly he felt for me and my family. Graciously, he pledged to be "available to do anything you request of me." What a warm and, I thought at the time, heartfelt letter.

Before I could pen a response, the *New York Times* reported Simon's unsolicited $17.50 offer for Taubman Centers' shares. Either David Simon hadn't shared his hostile intentions with his father (who is cochairman of the Simon Property's board), or Mel's letter was a shamefully disingenuous communication. The only other explanation is that his son's reckless strategy had left Mel feeling guilty and embarrassed. I'd like to give Mel the benefit of the doubt.

The Simon offer was pathetically low and easy to reject. Our five independent directors—S. Parker Gilbert, Jerome Chazen, Allan Bloostein, Peter Karmanos, and Graham Allison—were certainly no shrinking violets. Parker is a former chairman of Morgan Stanley; Jerry headed Liz Claiborne, Inc.; Alan was vice-chairman of May Department Stores; Peter founded one of the most successful high-tech companies on the planet (Compuware); and Graham built Harvard's Kennedy School into an international academic powerhouse. In addition, Taubman Centers' chief financial officer, Lisa Payne, who had joined the company from a senior position at Goldman Sachs, brought valuable Wall Street experience to her role on the board.

But David Simon had done his homework. He rallied investors who owned stock in both Simon and Taubman to push for the fire sale acquisition of our premier properties—a portfolio that had outperformed Simon's centers for decades. Ignoring the interests of Taubman shareholders who owned no Simon stock (like me), this "coalition of the willing" wanted to use our company to strengthen the inconsistent Simon portfolio, which was heavy with underperforming, at-risk properties. When *Detroit Free Press* business columnist Tom Walsh looked up the largest owners of Simon and Taubman stock:

> I discovered they were mostly the same people . . . Most big investors with holdings in both Simon and Taubman owned much more Simon stock than they did Taubman stock . . . If Simon could acquire Taubman's upscale malls on the cheap, that would be a great deal for owners of Simon stock and a not-so-good deal for owners of Taubman stock.

But as Walsh noted, the obligations of the board were clear: "They must act to maximize the value of the company on whose board they serve."

The battle got very ugly. Simon and their attorneys threw every conceivable strategy at the wall—except offering fair value—to negate my family's voting rights and eliminate a formidable competitor. My son, who was prohibited by the Bureau of Prisons from discussing his business strategy with me while I was in Rochester, did an outstanding job keeping the company focused on its important work. Thanks to Bobby's leadership and all the employees' resolve, the company kept its eye on the ball. Simon's final offer of $20 per share was nowhere near even the most conservative estimates of the Taubman portfolio's asset value. After draining both companies' resources for eleven months, Simon, which had been joined in the battle by Australian-owned Westfield Properties, would ultimately withdraw its offer on October 8, 2003.

Ironically, the takeover fight shone a bright light on the extraordinary quality of the Taubman Centers portfolio and its development pipeline, while highlighting the vulnerability (and prohibitive cost) of Simon's growth through acquisition strategy. Since the ceasefire through January 2007, Taubman Centers' shares, which have traded as high as $60, have outperformed those of Simon Property Group. The market has emphatically vindicated the board's rejection of the inadequate Simon offer.

Martin (Marty) Cohen, president of Cohen & Steers, Inc.—one of the most vocal of institutional investors described by Tom Walsh as "cross-owning" shareholders—summed up the battle most succinctly in the October 9, 2003 *Wall Street Journal*:

> Martin Cohen . . . who had criticized Taubman Centers' outright rejection of the offer, said one irony is that shopping mall values have drifted upward since the hostile bid was announced last November—just as Robert Taubman, Taubman Centers' chairman and CEO, had insisted they would. "Bobby was right," Mr. Cohen said. "$20 was way too low."

It was frustrating to be unable to participate in the defense of our company. But it also gave me a sense of perspective. In a few months, I knew I would be leaving the prison and that I would return to my life. The company I had built was still intact. I had homes, a loving family, and friends to return to. The same couldn't be said for the vast majority of my fellow inmates. Make no mistake: there were plenty of bad guys inside—murderers, rapists, molesters—who should never be free again. I'm delighted that they have been separated from society. But I met so many young men who had lost everything, including the most productive years of their lives, for a single drug-related mistake. Sure, they deserved punishment, even jail time. But to lose your freedom for two decades? The punishment just doesn't fit the crime. While I try my best to block out the memories of my time in Rochester, I can't help but think about these abandoned young men every day.

Ben is one of those unfortunate young men. He was a great friend to me, and we got to know each other very well. We cooked together in the community recreation room. With a few key ingredients (you could buy fresh fruit once a week) and a microwave we created magnificent culinary delights. He had a terrific young family in suburban Cleveland before the police raided his home one night, roughed him up in front of his wife and children, and claimed they found drugs. Now everything is gone: his home, his wife, his family, his future. What a shame. I really believe Ben was set up. Even if he wasn't, to destroy this intelligent man's life in the name of punishment is disgusting. I'm hoping Ben can make it out and make a new start. If there is justice in this world, Ben will get the second chance he deserves.

There were many other interesting guys in the prison. Jim was a contractor, restaurant owner, and pilot from Jackson, Michigan. He ran afoul of the law when two gentlemen approached him and inquired about his pilot's license. They offered him the opportunity to fly commercially to Miami, where he would be provided with an airplane to fly to Jamaica. For up to $500,000 per run, he would pick up a shipment of marijuana, which would be loaded onto his plane by Jamaican police officers, to be delivered to another location in the Caribbean. Jim admitted to loving the rush he got every time he risked everything on these adventures.

Jim, a personable and talented guy, is out now and doing very well on the straight and narrow.

Another fellow inmate was formerly the chief of detectives in a major midwestern county. He had great stories and a wonderful family. They came to visit a lot, as did many of his former detectives! Justin Volpe, the young New York police officer found guilty of assisting in the brutal treatment of Abner Louima, was serving time in Rochester. I met his very nice family during several visits (they're all paying for his terrible mistake).

The facility had several buildings. One held the inmates with serious psychiatric problems. For most of the day and evening hours, these challenged souls were isolated from the rest of the population. But at lunch, we all came together in the mess hall. On several occasions, a character known as Chainsaw made it a point to sit with me. He was very intelligent and loved to talk politics. He had a particular dislike for George W. Bush and expressed it with vigor. After a few of these political science sessions with Chainsaw, I asked around as to the origins of his colorful nickname. Apparently, he had been a successful restaurateur. Business took a turn for the worse, however, when he murdered two customers, chopped them up with a chainsaw, and served them as hamburger to his unsuspecting clientele. I made every effort to avoid him at lunch, and I was thankful he never learned that I had owned A&W.

Another guy—who actually was a talented commercial artist—made wine by fermenting orange juice in a hollowed-out portion of a wall hidden by a picture in his room. I put him to sleep drunk one night after hearing him staggering down the hall. (Eventually they caught him and threw him in the brig.) And then there was the very diminutive Jewish bank robber from Chicago. He stood just shy of five feet tall and had a mild humpback. After getting to know him, I suggested that he may have picked the wrong line of work. He was too short to see over the teller's counter.

The Jewish bank robber organized Friday night services for us. We didn't have the required ten to form minyan, but with the help of Larry, a Catholic dentist–drug dealer from Philadelphia (I think he was married to a Jew), we did our best. Larry was also a great bridge player and single-handedly organized our book club. *Seabiscuit* was by far our favorite selection. Faith, along with friends and family, can get you through the most difficult of life's tests. I found great strength and comfort in our tiny community and improvised religious services.

Another favorite pastime in prison, as you might imagine, was watching television, especially Court TV. Each floor had a recreation room where fifty to sixty guys fought over the remote. One day a few months into my stay, Dominick Dunne aired a Court TV special on the Sotheby's-Christie's scandal. Like so many of these cable shows, it played over and over again. So much for my strategy to keep a low profile! Come to think of it, it was shortly after Dominick's exposé that my roommate came up with his adoption proposal!

On May 15, 2003, nine and a half months after walking into the guardhouse of the Federal Medical Center in Rochester, Minnesota, the warden escorted me out the back, through a loading dock (he didn't want to give the news photographers a good shot, either) to meet my wife and son Bobby. Before I knew it, it was wheels up on the Gulfstream IV. I had lost a chunk of my life, my good name, and around twenty-seven pounds.

I had served my time for others; people going about their lives in New York and London who had initiated, executed, and lied about a serious crime for which they would receive little or no punishment.

About a year after I left Rochester, I received a letter from Daniel P. Davidson, who had served as the U.S. chairman of Christie's during the years the two houses colluded, which confirmed my take on the matter. He had read Christopher Mason's *The Art of the Steal* and wanted me to know that while he had not been a "principal player" at Christie's, he had been aware of some of what was going on in his company. As an insider, he concluded that "the real villains in the story were never punished—indeed some of them were rewarded."

Surprisingly, I felt no bitterness as we winged our way toward Detroit. After all, I was headed home to my family, friends, and community.

I had never felt so blessed.

~ EIGHTEEN ~

Coming Home

When I returned to Detroit from Rochester, Judge Damon Keith and Max Fisher organized a welcome-home luncheon for me at the Detroit Athletic Club that I will never forget. Everyone was there, from Mayor Kwame Kilpatrick and University of Michigan president Mary Sue Coleman, to former Michigan governor Jim Blanchard, business leaders, friends, family, and colleagues. What a great feeling to know that so many people had stood by me through such horrific trials and tribulations.

Of course, my reentry into society was also accompanied by some not-so-pleasant encounters. In December 2003, I attended a holiday party in the Manhattan home of my friend Ben Lambert (who had assisted us with the Irvine Ranch). As I was sitting in the library of Ben's beautiful apartment, David Simon approached me with his hand extended. I didn't stand up or shake his hand. But I did offer this special holiday greeting:

"You're a stupid little asshole."

To his credit, David turned and without a word disappeared into another room.

At my age, I don't buy green bananas. But I'm still taking the long view, looking at things and thinking how to make them both different and better. In my apartment building in New York, I recently rode the elevator with my neighbor, the Broadway director Harold Prince. He said, "I'm so retired." And I responded: "That's not the attitude. The attitude is that you're alive and you're better than you ever were. You're smarter, and you're better than you ever were. Don't think of yourself as old. You're experienced."

You have to take the long view. And when I do, I still see great opportunity for my industry and for my hometown. People wonder if the country has too many shopping centers. Well, the demographers tell me that by 2025 we'll have 70 million more people living in America than we have today. That's pretty astounding when you think about it. They'll all need a place to shop. And, no, I don't think they'll be buying everything online. On a macro level, sales of department store–type merchandise in 2006 totaled more than $1.0 trillion. By most estimates, total online sales for everything—not just DSTM—in 2006 barely passed the $100 billion mark. As for fashion items, the numbers over the Internet are even weaker. Sales in Taubman Centers properties (centers open at least one year) increased more than 7 percent in 2006. So, despite the popular perception, cyber sales are not getting an edge on brick-and-mortar business.

The technical limitations of computer screens make it impossible to effectively communicate such important product characteristics as fit, color, and feel. There are no fitting rooms or tailors in cyberspace. And the more expensive an article of clothing, the more critical it is that it fit well. There are an infinite number of colors and shades, and each works differently for each individual, depending on hair color, complexion, and eye color—even with high-quality print catalogues, the four-color process cannot match the exact color of a garment. There are no tactile experiences in cyberspace; at least not yet.

It is also ironic that one of the Web's greatest strengths is also one of its most serious weaknesses when it comes to retailing. Internet surfers can "drill down," as they say, to learn anything and every-thing about a product or service from the comfort of their homes. You would think that would build confidence. But without the guid-ance and persuasiveness of a salesperson, the hunt for information online tends to be endless. It's pretty easy to talk yourself out of a purchase when you can sit for hours reading negative product re-views (some legitimate, some not) and chatting with other buyers who are just as confused and uncertain as you are. Never underesti-mate the value of a knowledgeable salesperson.

That's not to say that the Internet is not a powerful force in re-tailing. Just like every other major business, retailing has harnessed the Web for manufacturing, supply-chain, fulfillment, and record-keeping functions. And successful retailers are pursuing multichan-nel distribution strategies, developing what some have called 360-degree marketing strategies. Customers can research a product online, come to a mall to purchase the item, and receive regular up-dates from the manufacturer via the Internet. Manufacturers like Sony and Apple—whose products do very well online—are enjoy-ing great success with offline showcase stores in Taubman malls.

Clearly, of all offerings, commodity products do best on the Web. If you've jogged every morning in the same size Nike running shoes, there is no reason why you can't reorder online (at least until Nike introduces a new model or your feet change). Purchases of books, CDs, and cell phones are strong (although the brick-and-mortar outlets of Borders and Barnes & Noble have never been stronger). With these products, the Web serves as a fulfillment vehicle, more than a promotional tool. And look who is doing best over the Inter-net: established brands. Consumers have confidence ordering from trusted merchants they have come to know in America's shopping centers.

The Internet retail revolution will occur when television view-ers are able to order goods right off the screen during prime-time programming. A blouse worn by one of the cast members of *Desperate Housewives* catches your eye. You click on the character and up comes a description of the item along with ordering information. Your computer knows your size and your credit card number. You click and the blouse is on its way. Technology experts call this "convergence." I call it *impulse* buying!

The technology, which is very close to being perfected, will take a bigger bite out of on-premises retailing. No question. But for now, when it comes to women's sportswear, shoes, men's dress slacks, and fancy wastebaskets, the strongest fashion statements are still being made in the best department and specialty stores.

Malls aren't dinosaurs. And neither is another great twentieth century economic force that people have been writing off: Detroit.

Wherever I go in the world, I'm proud to tell people I'm from Detroit. Even the halfway house I was assigned to in Detroit for the first weeks after leaving Rochester looked good to me.

Like me, Detroit has seen its share of success and failure, ups and downs. It gave mobility to the masses and has given the world an extraordinary number of talented people in a broad range of fields, from manufacturing to entertainment.

In many ways, Detroit's patterns of industrialization, suburbanization, and social diversity reflect America's journey from frontier to industrial powerhouse to nation in economic transition. Detroit faces challenges in part because geographic and economic forces have been at work for centuries to discourage density of development.

It starts with the water. The Great Lakes hold 18 percent of the planet's fresh water. Detroit's strategic location along the "straits" connecting these enormous bodies of water brought the fur traders in the eighteenth century and helped deliver the raw materials for the automobile industry in the twentieth century. The Detroit River has also created a boundary and barrier, defining the course of the city's growth. Development from the earliest days of human habitation has pushed out from the river over a 180-degree, not 360-degree, radius.

The land that stretches out from the river is very flat, with little variance in elevation. That made it easy to build roads, extend infrastructure, and get around fast, which in turn encouraged what we today call sprawl. In the early 1900s, Detroit was the automotive industry's equivalent to today's Silicon Valley. Young Detroit inventors and entrepreneurs like Henry Ford and Ransom Olds needed smooth roadways to sell their early models. In 1909, the one-mile stretch of Detroit's Woodward Avenue between Six Mile and Seven Mile Roads became the first road in the world to be paved with concrete. Concrete paving was cheaper and quicker to put down than cobblestone or brick, and much smoother. This breakthrough helped fuel the growth of the automobile industry and of the region. You could live in the suburbs and work in the city without having to depend on public transportation.

Then came the people. Thanks to Henry Ford, hundreds of thousands of workers and their families arrived from all over the world, seeking the extraordinary salary of $5 per day. When the board of directors of the Ford Motor Company announced this wildly generous pay policy—more than twice the amount of the average worker's compensation—on January 5, 1914, the *Wall Street Journal* accused Henry Ford of "economic blunders if not crimes." It dubbed the $5 day "the most foolish thing ever attempted in the industrial world."

Of course we know that the policy in many ways ushered in the age of the American middle class. Workers became *customers*. They were able to own their own cars, buy their own homes, and pay taxes to municipalities building public schools that could send generations on to college and success. Thousands of these Ford workers were African Americans who migrated from the South to start a new life with their families. Thanks to this migration and the competitive wages, Detroit—while not always a perfect place to live for African Americans—developed a strong African American middle class.

By 1925, Detroit boasted the highest per capita income and the highest percentage of home ownership in the world. But this wage-driven revolution had unintended consequences. Traditional business institutions like banks and insurance companies, which were dependent upon large workforces, could not compete for labor against Ford Motor Company's wages. These essential white-collar institutions, along with the massive office buildings required to house their employees, did not flourish in Detroit. Cleveland, Chicago, Pittsburgh, and other midwestern cities, which were less dominated by the auto industry, developed more balanced economies and more dense downtown business districts with banks and insurance companies clustered within walking distance of one another.

The manufacturing plants of Detroit were not similarly clustered. The river and the rail lines brought iron ore from Lake Superior and the coal from Lake Erie to massive industrial campuses built along or within a short distance of the Detroit River. Workers had the income to afford their own homes near the plants, resulting in low-density housing patterns throughout the region. Ford's 2,000-acre River Rouge plant, designed by Albert Kahn and located three miles inland from the Detroit River, helped establish the character of Detroit land development. *Vanity Fair* in 1928 called it "the most significant public monument in America." This self-contained industrial complex included a foundry, glass plant, tire plant, assembly building, cement plant, power house, pressed steel building, miles of roadway, and one hundred miles of railway track. At its peak of production, the Rouge plant employed 100,000 people.

With the innovation of the production line, Kahn's Rouge plant was the world's first single-level, horizontal manufacturing building. It replaced the vertical factory model—like Ford's Highland Park, Michigan, plant—that relied on gravity to ease and speed production.

Albert Kahn was commissioned to design the Fisher Building, which opened in 1928 across Grand Boulevard from General Motors headquarters. At that time, the GM structure was the largest office building in the world. But the Fisher and GM buildings were not built downtown. Detroit's planners envisioned and encouraged a three-mile corridor of growth along Woodward Avenue from the river to what became known as the New Center area. The theory was that development would spread along this corridor. And to be fair, neighborhoods of cultural, medical, and academic institutions did spring up.

With few banks and insurance companies demanding office space, it was unrealistic to expect the pattern of commercial development in Detroit to extend three miles up Woodward, but the planners never gave up on the idea. They kept encouraging growth in the outlying New Center area. Detroit's hoped-for extension of dense commercial development from the river to the New Center area never materialized. And it never will (at least not in my lifetime).

During the war years we were among the most prosperous and fastest-growing cities in the world. With peace, Detroit helped fuel the nation's prosperity and answered America's call for mobility. Along with the baby boom came an auto boom, and Detroit benefited economically as much as any city in the nation. Detroit and Detroiters were spreading out, and retail followed the flow of population. Remember those massive stores that Hudson's built in Detroit's suburbs? They destroyed the competitive opportunity within the region for the chain's historic flagship store downtown. Every line of merchandise was available in depth in the more convenient suburban stores. Another reason to "go downtown" was gone. Hudson's suburban strategy certainly hastened this landmark's demise and forever changed the retail landscape in Detroit.

In the 1970s, I made deals with JCPenney and Lord & Taylor to come to the Detroit metro area and anchor five projects—four suburban centers (Fairlane Town Center, Twelve Oaks, Lakeside, and Briarwood) and the proposed Cadillac Square development downtown. The historic Hudson's store was to be the centerpiece of Cadillac Square, but a misguided young architect from the firm of Smith, Hinchman & Grylls scuttled the project with the help of some equally misguided preservationists in Washington, D.C. To save two insignificant structures on Griswald Street (both of which are still boarded up), Hudson's and the city's downtown retail vitality were cheated out of a second lease on life. The store was closed in the mid-1980s and torn down in the late 1990s.

People moved out of Detroit for all the reasons of geography, economics, and personal taste that we've been discussing. And they moved out because of the growing racial tension that exploded in 1967. The tragic Detroit riots of 1967, and the festering social problems they reflected, influenced the course of Detroit's development as much as any street patterns, business decisions, or geography. Detroit's population peaked in 1953 at around 2 million. By 1970, it had declined by a half million people. The 2000 United States census found only 950,000 people living in Detroit—a decline in just fifty years of 1 million people.

I can think of only one comparable example in history of such rapid urban population decline. Vienna, Austria, at the beginning of the twentieth century had much in common with Detroit. This bustling European city—the capital of the Austro-Hungarian Empire—was a center of arts, education, government, and finance. And like Detroit at its peak, it was home to more than 2 million people.

But the twentieth century was not kind to Vienna. The Hapsburg empire fell with the outbreak of World War I, and the city's diplomatic infrastructure disappeared overnight. By 1950, after World War II and the Allied occupation, the city's population had fallen to just over 1 million, a decline of 50 percent.

What's interesting is how Vienna is dealing today with such

traumatic change. While large sections of the city, where beautiful homes once stood, are vacant and waiting for redevelopment, Vienna's historic strengths—the opera, museums, and restaurants—are among the finest in the world. City leaders are investing in the aspects of the city that remain internationally attractive and competitive. Tourists continue to visit, trade is flourishing, and people are slowly but surely moving back to the city. Population has climbed back up to more than 1.5 million people.

We're hoping there is a second act for Detroit as well. Following the disastrous 1967 riots, I was one of the members of the business community who formed Detroit Renaissance. Along with my friends Max Fisher and Henry Ford II, we committed time, influence, and resources to rebuild the economic strength of our great but wounded city. I headed the organization's development committee and had the honor to work with Mayors Coleman Young and Dennis Archer in planning several of Detroit's most important projects, including the Cobo Hall convention hall expansion and the beautiful new Comerica Park baseball stadium.

If Detroit is going to be able to attract residents downtown, it must look to the riverfront for regionally competitive housing. The Riverfront Apartments, which Max Fisher and I helped develop in the early 1980s, may not have been my best real estate investment. But it laid some of the groundwork for Detroit's exciting Riverwalk initiative, spearheaded by General Motors, the Kresge Foundation, and the city. The suburbs don't have a comparable amenity, and it is absolutely essential that we reclaim the riverfront from its industrial past.

Other market-rate housing is being developed in Detroit, thanks to dedicated hometown developers like Cullen DuBose. My friend Cullen has created a wonderful community of affordable single-family homes directly adjacent to our world-class museum, the Detroit Institute of Arts. The units sold out quickly and are anchoring an attractive, prospering part of our city.

General Motors' decision in 1996 to adopt Detroit's Renaissance Center as its world headquarters has also been one of the most positive events in the history of Detroit. Their presence and commitment to downtown has already paid extraordinary dividends. Unfortunately, even General Motors can't move the Renaissance Center off the river a few blocks, where it should have been built in the first place. My friend Henry Ford II was the driving force behind the development of the RenCen in the 1970s. I was one of the city's lone voices in opposition to the project's location and design. I remember driving by the construction site one day with Henry. He wanted my advice on some last-minute design issues. "Henry," I said, "fill in the hole." The massive towers, as impressive as they are, stand in isolation from the city's central business district, blocking access to the river and diminishing the opportunity for residential development along the water. But General Motors has made important physical changes to the complex, revitalized the center's retail offerings, and injected magnificent new life into our city.

Taubman Centers board member Peter Karmanos, founder of Compuware, also deserves accolades for bringing his energy and company headquarters downtown. The Ilitch family (owners of Little Caesars Pizza, the Detroit Tigers, and Red Wings) has reenergized our sports and entertainment offerings. And the Fords have brought the Lions back home in a beautiful new world-class sports facility (Ford Field), host to the 2006 NFL Super Bowl.

And there are many other heroes—developers, investors, and independent business owners—working to revitalize Detroit. We will fail, however, if we continue to measure Detroit's success only in terms of its size. Let's be honest, brutally honest.

We don't have to be one of the ten largest cities in America (a distinction we surrendered in 2005) to be one of the best cities in America. We don't have to preserve the city's archaic street grid and restricted residential lot patterns designed a century ago to accommodate 2 million people. Wherever there are neighborhoods of abandoned homes, we should be willing to redirect streets and configure residential lots to be competitive with the land offerings in the suburbs. Why not build a golf course surrounded by homes where dense neighborhoods of row houses once stood? Many cities would be well served by such a creative approach.

There also is an increasing understanding that the Detroit metropolitan area, which reaches well beyond the city limits, is a diverse market of over five million people blessed with a variety of occupational and lifestyle choices. Ann Arbor, Novi, Southfield, Dearborn, Troy, and Detroit are in a very real sense "edge cities" comprising a twenty-first-century metropolis as attractive, diverse, and competitive as any in the nation.

Will Detroit and its downtown play a special role in this region? Of course.

Southfield will never host a Super Bowl. There is no place in Troy to study an historic Diego Rivera mural (we have one at the Detroit Institute of Arts). There will be only one Hard Rock Cafe in the region (we have one with plenty of Motown memorabilia in the Compuware building downtown). And if you want to watch a beautiful sunset along the Detroit River from the comfort of the Riverfront Apartments, you have to live downtown.

In recent years, I've been personally involved with many of the efforts. My friend Max Fisher used to say that there are three ways an individual can contribute to organizations and community initiatives: you can give your money, your time, and your good name. I've made a practice of giving all three. Since 1980, I have made personal charitable contributions of more than $125 million. But my greatest satisfaction comes from giving my time and expertise, and in recent years I've been focused on ways to make institutions in Detroit different and better. With the help of my good friend and extraordinary architect Michael Graves (working with the Detroit-based Smith-

Group), we are creating a much more efficient and welcoming home for the Detroit Institute of Arts' world-class collections. I've helped plan the new internal circulation patterns at the DIA. (You could say we are breaking down threshold resistance!) I am also honored to serve on the board and chair the building committee of Detroit's College for Creative Studies, a unique institution that is effectively training the next generation of artists and automotive designers. And in April 2006, we dedicated the A. Alfred Taubman Student Services Center at Lawrence Technological University in South-field—where I learned many of the architectural and planning skills I use every day.

Like any great city's, Detroit's past is full of triumphs and trage-dies. We will no doubt continue to struggle with change and oppor-tunity. But from my vantage point, I see plenty of greatness still ahead of this special city—my hometown.

And of course, the Detroit area remains a great place to do busi-ness. That little company I started with my father, some big dreams, and a $5,000 loan, is still based in Bloomfield Hills. It has grown into a large enterprise, with twenty-three centers, five hundred employees, and an equity capitalization of $4.5 billion as of January 2007. I own almost one-third of it but am mostly an observer. The management team, led by Robert Taubman, runs it better than I ever did. We're still developing, still creating exciting new retail environments, and still breaking down threshold resistance. One of our current projects is a retail, office, and residential complex in downtown Salt Lake City. Who would have thought a Jewish guy from Detroit and the Church of Latter-Day Saints would be business partners.

Only in America!

- EPILOGUE -

Over my lifetime I've gotten pretty good at assessing and responding to threshold resistance. It's a skill that serves you well in business and life. Over the last eight decades, I've enjoyed great success and experienced gut-wrenching personal failure. But through it all I've stayed positive, always seeing opportunity in even the toughest challenges.

Breaking down barriers is very rewarding. It can be scary and risky. It can also be fun. Bringing exciting new shopping opportunities to communities across America was great fun, as was opening the stimulating world of art and collectibles to broader audiences around the world. Solving building design issues in Baku, winning a football championship, watching a youngster enjoy a root beer float, and looking out over thousands of acres of smart new development along the Pacific Ocean are terrific experiences—especially for an awkward but motivated kid from Pontiac, Michigan.

Every success involved placing opportunities in front of customers, offering value, and providing an enriching, entertaining experience. Figuring out how to make things better, not just different, is the first step in any business plan. For whatever reason, it came naturally to me to look at things differently. But it's something you have to work on and became accustomed to doing. And success always leads to greater confidence.

You'll always face resistance. In fact, the better your idea, the more some people will want you to fail. Believe in yourself, and you're on your way.

As I look back over my life, my family, without a doubt, has been my proudest accomplishment. They're terrific. They're also why I wrote this book. Everyone, of course, is welcome to read my thoughts. But I had a very specific audience in mind as I tackled this project: my nine grandchildren.

These lessons and reflections are for my daughter Gayle Kalisman's two sons. Jason, continue embracing life and your skyrocketing career at Goldman Sachs. And Philip, with your PhD in chemistry from Berkeley, you'll be the first scientist in the family—and hopefully our first Nobel laureate.

My son Robert will have to buy at least four books for his sons and daughter. Alexander Alfred, as you continue your studies at Harvard University, get over to the Taubman Center as often as possible. And Ghislaine, Theodore, and Sebastian, I hope when you're old enough to read your grandfather's musings, you'll put down *Harry Potter* and give me a chance.

My son William's children, Oliver and Abigail, may want to read my book with their father. It's okay to ask your dad to explain some of the stuff about the art world.

And I hope my stepdaughter Tiffany's beautiful young girl, Tatiana, already multilingual like her grandmother, will enjoy hearing about my international experiences. Who knows; the book may someday be translated into Azerbaijani.

Jason, Philip, Alexander, Ghislaine, Theodore, Sebastian, Oliver, Abigail, and Tatiana, now you know a whole lot more about "Pops."

INDEX

A&W Great Food Restaurant units, 59, 60
A&W Restaurants, x, 58–63, 98, 109, 116, 117, 127, 139, 184
    advertising of, 62–63
    brand image of, 58
    hot dogs of, 60, 61
    marketing failures of, 62–63
    purchase price of, 58–59
    resale of, 63
    in shopping centers and malls, 60–61, 63
A&W Root Beer, 58, 61, 63, 143
Acquavella, Bill, 107, 146
advertising, 62, 74, 100
    of A&W Restaurants, 62–63
    of department stores, 33, 68
    television, 112
African Americans, 155–56, 176, 191–92
Agnelli, Giovanni, 100
Agree, Charles N., vii–ix, 8, 10, 11
AIDS, 132
Ainslie, Michael, 96–97, 137–39
Albert J. Frankel Co., 20
Albright, Burl, 68
Allen, Charles, Jr., 46, 48, 51–55
Allen, Herb, 46
Allen, Roy, 58
Allied Stores, 21
Allison, Graham, 131, 180–81
amyotrophic lateral sclerosis (ALS), 132
Andy Warhol Collection, 107
anti-trust laws, 141–42, 143, 150, 167–68
Arborland mall, 13
arcades, 26–28, 72
Archer, Dennis, 195
Arnault, Bernard, 148
Aronson, Arnold, 71, 72
art, 38
    pop, 117
    root beer and, 110, 111, 116–17
    stolen, 101
    Taubman's collection of, 6, 84, 101, 103
art auctions, *see* Christie's; Sotheby's

art dealers, professional, 84, 88, 97, 101–5, 106, 107
art market, 87–88, 97, 146
Art of the Steal, The (Mason), 151–52, 154, 157–58, 169, 186
art press, 92, 104, 105, 162
art registry, international, 101
Ashcroft, John, 179
Asia Pacific markets, 60
AT&T, 127
Athena Group, 124–26
Azerbaijan, 125
azidothymidine (AZT), 132

Bacon, Francis, 84
Baker, Samuel, 85, 136
Baku, Azerbaijan, 125, 199
Ballard, Claude, 52
Bank of America, 51, 54
banks, 31, 32, 50, 51
Barbara Ann Karmanos Cancer Institute, 132
Baron, Ronald S., 66–67
bazaars, oriental, 26
Beaux-Arts school of architecture, 6
Bellamy, Richard, 84
Best of Everything, The (Marion), 104
Beverly Center, 120
Beyer Blinder Belle, 79
Bithell, Tom, 114
Blanchard, Jim, 128, 187
Bloomingdale's, 33, 67, 69 71, 72, 74–75, 106, 120
Bloostein, Allan, 180–81
Boardman, Dixon, 125
Boies, David, 151–52
Bond, Alan, 104–5
Borbón, Infanta Pilar de, Duchess of Badajoz, 100
Borovik, Artyom, 126
brand images, 21
    at A&W, 58
    of department stores, 65, 71

brand images (*continued*)
  in fashion merchandising, 77–78, 79, 80, 82
  off-price outlets and, 81–83
  of Sotheby's, 86
  of Trump, 79
  of Wal-Mart, 78
Brandt, Ralph, 124
Brazil, 135
Bren, Donald, 51, 54, 55
Brio Tuscan Grille, 59
Broadway Stores, 21
Brooks, Diana "Dede," 97, 144–45, 162, 163
  Ainslie's absences tracked by, 138
  appropriate punishment avoided by, 171, 185–86
  as CEO, 140
  in collusion on commission schedules, 145 146–48, 151, 152, 154, 165
  false testimony of, 145, 147, 148, 164–65
  "flipper" lawyer hired by, 150, 171
  Taubman's misplaced trust in, 138–40, 146–47, 170
  unauthorized sale offer of, 148
Brown University, 131
Brunton, Gordon, 87, 90–91, 92
Bucksbaum, Martin and Matthew, 20
Burger King, 57
Burke, O. W., construction company, ix, 11
Burlington Arcade, 27
Burlington Coat Factory Warehouse, 67
Bush v. Gore, 151
business precepts, 109–12, 117–18
Business Week, 174
  family businesses articles of, 122, 123
  Taubman in, 33, 40

Cadillac Fairview Corporation, 51, 52
California, 14, 15–24, 39, 46, 58, 115, 120
  see also Irvine Ranch, purchase of
California Pizza Kitchen, 59
Camoys, Lord, 164
Canada, 20, 51
cancer research, 132
Carrington, Lord, 141
Carter, Anthony, 114, 115, 117
Castelli, Leo, 84
celebrity auction sales, 106–7
Central Intelligence Agency, 155–56
Charlston Place, 79, 121
charter schools, 129–30
Chase Manhattan Bank, 24, 43, 51, 92, 135
Chazen, Jerome, 180–81

Cheesecake Factory, 59
Chicago, Ill., 18, 21, 23–24, 28, 33
Chicago Symphony Orchestra, 44
China, 124
Christie's, 86, 88, 89, 104, 107
  disclosure of guarantees at, 144
  French acquisition of, 147
  management transition of, 141
  Sotheby's relationship with, 141, 142, 143–45
  see also Sotheby's-Christie's price-fixing scandal
"Chunnel" project, joke about, 11
Churchill, Sir Winston, 136–37
Cigar Aficionado, 106–7
Coach, 77
coat buyers, 68
Coats, Williams, 129
Cogan, Marshall, 87, 90, 92
Colasuonno, Lou, 150
Coldwell Banker, 16
Coleman, Mary Sue, 187
collecting, popularity of, 107
Comerica, 10, 46
commodities businesses, 78–79
comparison shopping, 34
Concise Townscape, The (Cullen), 35
Concord, Calif., 16, 22
conscious parallelism, legal concept of, 142
consistent mediocrity, 57, 60, 61
corsages, wholesale, 7–8
Costco, 83
Coste, Pascal, 26
Courting Justice (Boies), 151, 152
covenants of operation, 43
Crate and Barrel, 76
credit, 33, 84, 103, 104–5
"cross-shopping," 32
Cullen, George, 34–35
Curiel, François, 154
Cushman & Wakefield, 46
customer service, 68, 69, 70–71

Daniels, Judge George B., 163–73
  Adam Smith quote allowed by, 166–67
  delayed judicial decisions of, 172–73
  instructions to the jury of, 167–68
  motions repeatedly denied by, 163–64
  at sentencing hearing, 170–71
Davenport, Iowa, 1–2
Davidge, Christopher, 141, 144–45
  amnesty granted to, 153–55

in collusion on commission schedules, 145, 148, 150, 152, 153–55, 165
  false testimony of, 157–58, 164–65
  Tennant's "memo" stolen by, 158
Davidson, Daniel P., 185–86
Davis Polk & Wardwell, 149–50
Dayton's, 18
DeBartolo, Edward J., 20, 21
department stores, 10, 12, 15–23, 64–72, 104, 142, 190
  advertising of, 33, 68
  anchor, 13, 16, 19, 23, 33–34, 36, 43, 59, 66, 67, 71–72, 73, 120–21, 193–94
  as arcades, 27–28
  bargain basements of, 82, 83
  brand images of, 65, 71
  customer confidence in, 64–65, 71
  customer service of, 68, 69, 70–71
  as dinosaurs, 64, 71
  downtown locations of, 16–19, 21, 32, 33, 34, 82, 193
  fashion, 73–75
  full-line, 73
  influence of, 18
  as large employers, 18
  name brand distribution controlled by, 18, 98
  "one piece for all" in, 28
  as "people pumps," 33, 72
  retail competitors excluded by, 18–19, 98
  retail industry changes and, 69–70
  suburban branch stores of, 16–17, 18–19, 82
department-store-type merchandise (DSTM), 73, 188
Detroit, Mich., vii, xi, 13–14, 15–16, 18, 25, 45, 50, 124, 128, 131, 190–98
  African Americans in, 191–92
  College for Creative Studies of, 198
  developmental history of, 190–94
  Eastern Market of, 7–8
  future development of, 195–98
  metropolitan area of, 197
  1967 riots in, 194, 195
  Renaissance Center of, 196
  riverfront housing in, 127–28, 195
  Rosa Parks incident in, 172
Detroit Bank and Trust, 46
Detroit Free Press, 91, 181
Detroit Institute of Arts, 84, 195, 197, 198
Detroit Lions football team, 113, 196
Detroit Medical Center, 132
Detroit Renaissance, 195

Dillard's, 71
discount stores, 4, 67–68, 69, 80–83
Dornbrook, Thom, 114
Dreamer, The (Modigliani), 116
drugstores, 10
DuBose, Cullen, 195–96
Dunleavy, Steve, 169
Dunne, Dominick, 162, 170–71, 185
Durant, Lydell, 168–69

Eastdil Realty, 50
Eastridge shopping center, 20, 23
education, 62, 128–31
  charter schools in, 129–30
  corporate importance of, 130–31
  higher, 129, 131
  high schools, 95–96, 114, 129
  teachers in, 129, 130
E. J. Korvette, 81
Emerson, Ralph Waldo, 61
Emporium Capwell, 16
Engler, John, 129
entrepreneurs, 2, 12, 58, 61
  creativity of, 10
  difference in, 9–10, 199–200
  optimism of, 10
ESPN, 112
ethics, professional, 139–40

Fairlane Town Center, 45
fair-trade laws, 141–42
family businesses, 11–12, 121–27, 179–80
fascia treatments, 14
fashion department stores, 73–75
fashion merchandising, 73–83, 188
  in bathrooms and kitchens, 76–77
  brand image in, 77–78, 79, 80, 82
  in commerce revolution, 74–75
  democratization of, 76–77
  good design in, 74–77, 88
  mass merchandising vs., 74, 77–78, 80
  off-price outlets and, 80–83
  price in, 75–77
  taste in, 75, 77
  utility vs., 75
  Wal-Mart question and, 77, 80
Federal Express, 111–12
Federal Medical Center, 174–86
Federal's, 11–12, 13
Federated Stores, 69–70
Feldman, Eva, 132
Field, Marshall, 28, 65

Finkelstein, Ed, 69–70
Fisher, Marjorie, 124
Fisher, Max, 13–14, 51, 55, 57–58, 92, 113, 115,
    121, 124, 127–28, 139, 140, 147, 172, 178,
    187, 195, 197, 198
Fisher Building, 193
Fiske, Robert, 149–50, 165–66, 171
Flint, Mich., 13
Fluor, Simon, 48
fluorescent lighting, outdoor, 14
Flutie, Doug, 115
food franchises, 56–63
    see also A&W Restaurants
football, professional, 109, 112–16
Ford, Henry, 74, 191
Ford, Henry, II, 51, 55, 86, 92, 121, 122, 140, 195,
    196
Ford Motor Company, 2, 51, 122, 191–93
Forrester, Glenn, 169
Fortune, 117, 149
France, 144, 147
    arcades of, 26–27, 72
free-trade rulings, 18
frozen food distribution business, 57, 62

Gaede, Keith, 48
Galeries de Bois of Palais Royal, 26–27
Galleria Vittorio Emanuele II, 27
General Felt Industries, 90
General Growth Properties, 20
General Motors, 127, 193, 195, 196
General Motors Pension Trust, 126, 127
Getty, Ann, 100
Getty, Gordon, 122–23
Getty, J. Paul, 123
Getty Museum, 105, 122
Getty Oil Company, 122–23
Gilbert, S. Parker, 180–81
Gioia, Emilio, 92, 124
Gladwell, Malcolm, 25
Goldman Sachs, 52, 67, 181
golf courses, golfing, 4, 6, 66, 79–80, 107–8,
    112, 197
Gordon, Sheldon, 16, 120
Graham, Katharine, 70
Grand Rapids, Mich., 23
Granholm, Jennifer, 155
Graves, Michael, 76, 77, 197
Great Britain, 27, 60
    Monopolies and Mergers Commission of,
        92–93
    see also Sotheby's

Greater Detroit Chamber of Commerce,
    130–31, 139–40
Greene, John, 166–67
Green Galleries, 84
Gregory, Alexis, 92
Gruen, Victor, 25, 27
Gucci, 77
Guinier, Lani, 155–56
Gumm, Ira, viii

Hahn, Ernest W., 20, 21
H&M, 76
Harvard Business Review, 95
Harvard Business School, Taubman's lecture
    at, 109–18
    art and root beer linked in, 110, 111,
        116–17
    business precepts in, 109–12, 117–18
    journalistic accounts of, 116–17
    Modigliani painting in, 116
    needs satisfaction principle in, 110, 111–12,
        114, 116
    USFL in, 109, 112–16
Harvard University, 200
    Kennedy School of Government of, 131,
        181
Haviland, John, 27
Hayward, Calif., 16, 59–60
Hebert, Bobby, 114, 115
Henri, Bendel, 79
Highland Park, Mich., vii–ix
highways, 19, 21–22, 23–24
    restaurants on, 56–57, 58
Hindlip, Lord, 154
Hines, Gerald, 7
Hiroshima, Japan, 5
HIV infection, 132
Hoffman, Edwin, 66–69, 71, 72, 138
Holiday Inn motels, 57
Horwitz, Jerome, 132
hot dogs, 60, 61
"hot spots," 19
hours of operation, 28, 43, 59
Howard Johnson's, 56–57, 58
Hudson's, 15–16, 18, 19, 21, 193, 194
Hungarian sausages, 61

ice skating rinks, 70
Ilitch family, 196
I. Magnin, 67
impulse buying, 31, 32, 39, 44, 110, 190
Indiana, Robert, 84

International Council of Shopping Centers (ICSC) conventions, 142
International Paper, 54
Internet sales, 189–90
inventory risks, 89
Iran, 45
Irises (van Gogh), 104–5
Irvine, James, 46–47
Irvine, James, III, 47
Irvine, James "J. I.," II, 47, 48
Irvine, Myford, 47–48
Irvine Company, 47–55
    corporate earnings of, 49–50, 52–53
Irvine Ranch, purchase of, ix, 46–55, 119, 187
    appraisal and evaluation in, 49–50, 52
    bank consortium in, 50, 51
    bidding in, 50–53
    closing of, 53–54
    Mobil Oil and, 48–52
    offering agreement in, 53
    partners in, 51–52, 54–55, 92, 121
    professional relationships and, 44–46
    and ranch history, 46–48
    resale of, 54–55, 84–85
    residential ground leases in, 51, 52, 113
    revenues of, 54–55
    road and utility infrastructure in, 52
Istanbul, bazaars of, 26

James Irvine Foundation, 47, 48
Javits, Jacob, 131–32
JCPenney, 13, 16, 19, 21, 23, 71, 73, 193–94
jewelry stores, 81–82
Johns, Jasper, 84
Johnson, Charlie, 54
Justice Department, U.S., 146–60, 161–73
    amnesty program of, 153–56, 160
    art market probe of, 146
    Brooks as witness for, 147, 150
    Davidge as witness for, 157–58
    Tennant indicted by, 156–58, 160
    see also Taubman, A. Alfred, trial of

Kahn, Albert, 192–93
Kalisman, Gayle Taubman, 13, 85–86, 124, 162, 168, 200
Kalisman, Michael, 124
Karmanos, Peter, 180–81, 196
Kaufman, Steven, 150
Keith, Judge Damon J., 155–56, 172, 187
Kilpatrick, Kwame, 187
Kissinger, Nancy, 179

Klutznick, Philip M., 20–21
Kmart, 74, 76–77
Knoll Group, 90
Kohl's, 21
Kohn Pedersen Fox, 79
Kolodney, Reva, *see* Taubman, Reva Kolodney
Korvette, E. J., 81
Kresge, S. S., 13
Kresge Foundation, 195
Kringle Bears promotion, 70–71
Kroger, 13
Kughn, Richard, 12, 13, 139–40

Lacey, Robert, 98
La Cumbre Plaza shopping center, 20
Lagerfeld, Karl, 76, 77
Lally, James, 97
Lakeside shopping center, 45
Lambert, Ben, 50, 187
land absorption projections, 50
land grants, Spanish, 46
land-use planning, 30, 48
Lanier, Judith, 129
Larson, Robert, 123, 124, 139
Lauder, Estée, 86
Lawrence Technological University, 198
Lazard, Frères, 126, 127
Lazarus, 18
Leona Group, The, 129–30
Leonardo da Vinci, 31, 36
LeRoy, Mervyn, 44
LeRoy, Warner, 44
Leventhal, Kenneth, 50
Like No Other Store . . . : The Bloomingdale's Legend and the Revolution in American Marketing (Traub), 74–75
Limited, The, 39, 45
Lindner, Carl, 57–58
Linemann, Peter, 7
Llewellyn, Graham, 98
locations, 30–41, 119–20
    of arcades, 27, 72
    downtown, 30–33
    impulse buying and, 31, 32, 39, 44
    "100 percent," 31, 32, 35–36, 37
    of service businesses, 31–32
    upscale, 77
    see also shopping centers and malls, design of
Lombardi, Vince, Jr., 115
Lopez, Carlos, 6
Lord & Taylor, 21, 193–94

Los Angeles, Calif., 120
Louima, Abner, 184
Louis Vuitton, 77
luxury retailers, 73, 75, 80, 88
    auction business as, 104
    see also fashion merchandising

McDonald's, 57, 58, 62–63
McGriff, Tyrone, 114
Macy's, 16, 17, 21–23, 65, 69–70, 71, 73, 121
magazine roads, 37
Mall at Short Hills, 120–21
Manufacturers National Bank of Detroit,
    10, 12, 51
Marcus, Stanley, 72
Marcuse, Melinda, 164, 178
Marguleas, Howard, 51
Marion, John, 97, 104
Marion, Louis, 97
Marshall Field's, 18, 21, 73
Marshalls, 82
Mason, Christopher, 151–52, 154,
    157–58, 169, 186
mass distribution, 81
mass merchandising, 74, 77–78, 80
    price in, 78
mass production, 28, 65, 76
Maxwell's Plum, 44
May Company, 23, 69
medical research, 132
Meier, Richard, 162–63
merchandising control, 38–39
Metcalfe, David, 85, 86
Michigan, University of, 4, 5–8, 10, 13, 66, 78,
    112, 113, 131, 132, 187
Michigan Cancer Foundation, 132
Michigan Panthers football team, 109, 112–16,
    119, 127
Michigan Partnership for New Education,
    128–30
Michigan State University (MSU), 128
Milan, Italy, 27
Milstein, Monroe, 67–68
Milstein brothers, 57–58
Milton Meyer Company, 16
Milwaukee, Wisc., 36
Minnesota Vikings football team, 115
Minor, Paul K., 159
Miro, Jeffrey, 90–92, 124, 138–39, 147, 175
Mobil Oil, 48–52
Modigliani, Amedeo, 116
Monaghan, Tom, 179

money-back guarantees, 28
Montgomery Ward, 13, 18, 21
Monuments modernes de la Perse (Coste), 26
mortgages, 2–3, 42–43
movie theaters, multiplex, 39
Mrs. Ray's Bridal Salon, 11–12
Mullen, David, 67, 69
Muller, Scott, 149–50, 164
Mulligan, Robert, 67
multichannel distribution strategies, retail,
    189–90
Municipal Arts Society, 79
Murray, Laura, 150

name brands, 18, 75, 98, 189
National Football League (NFL), 115–16
needs satisfaction, principle of, 110, 111–12,
    114, 116
Neiman Marcus, 67, 69, 71, 73, 75, 78, 81, 82,
    121
neon tubing, 14
New Jersey Generals football team, 115
New Orleans Saints football team, 115
New Yorker, 25, 153
New York Stock Exchange, 101
New York Times, 126–27, 172–73, 180
Nordstrom, 68, 69, 71, 82, 121
Northern Michigan University, 130
North Flint Plaza shopping center, 13
Northland Mall, 19

Oakland Invaders football team, 115
off-price outlets, 80–83
Ogilvy, David, 52
Ogilvy, Sir Angus, 100
oil industry, 14
Onassis, Jacqueline Kennedy, 79, 106–7
operating businesses, 78–79
Oppenheimer, 67, 124
Optima Fund, 125

Parke-Bernet, 97, 98
Park Forest, Ill., 21
parking, 13
    downtown, 31, 32, 34
    upper and lower, 36–37
Parks, Rosa, 172
Paseo Nuevo shopping center, 20
Payne, Lisa, 181
Payson, John Whitney, 104
Pennsylvania, University of, 7
Persia, 26

Persian carpets, 88
Peters, Jimmy, 46
Petrie, Milton J., vii–ix, 8, 39, 51, 55, 92, 106, 140
P.F. Chang's China Bistro, 59
Philadelphia, Pa., 7, 18, 28, 69
Philadelphia Arcade, 27
Philadelphia Stars football team, 114
Phillips, 148
Phillips, Diana, 100, 143
Phi Sigma Delta fraternity, 5
Phoenix, Ariz., 126
piazzas, 27
Pier 1 Imports, 76
Pillsbury, Don, 147, 149, 159
Pinault, François, 151, 154–55
Pinney, Ray, 114
Pitt, Bill, 92
Pittsburgh Steelers football team, 114
Polo, 77, 78
Pontiac, Mich., 1, 2–4, 11–13
Pontiac Silverdome stadium, 113
pop art, 117
Pottery Barn, 39, 76
price-fixing, see Sotheby's-Christie's price-fixing scandal
Prince, Harold, 188
product standardization, 28, 65, 76
Prudential Insurance Company, 120, 139
Pulitzer, Joseph, Jr., 126
Pulitzer Publishing Company, 126–27

Rauschenberg, Robert, 84
real estate development, 78–80
   by Athena Group, 124–26
   brochures of, 27
   of mixed-use projects, 79
   multiple property formats in, 79–80
   of office buildings vs. retail properties, 78–79
   Riverfront Apartments, 127–28, 172, 195, 198
real estate investing, 45–55
   see also Irvine Ranch, purchase of
reciprocal easement agreements, 43
Reif, Rita, 92
residential ground leases, 51, 52, 113
restaurants, 38, 95
   consistent mediocrity of, 57, 60, 61
   diners, 56
   downtown locations of, 31, 32
   on highways, 56–57, 58

in shopping centers and malls, 22, 59–61, 63, 72
   Sotheby's Café, 98–99
   see also A&W Restaurants
return policies, 28
Riley, Joseph P., Jr., 121
ring roads, 37
risk taking, 9–10
Riverfront Apartments, 127–28, 172, 195, 198
Robert Lurie Real Estate Center, 7
Rohatyn, Felix, 126
Roosevelt, Franklin, 21
root beer, 58, 61
   art and, 110, 111, 116–17
   as taste of British toothpaste, 60
root beer floats, 58, 199
Rose, Irving, 13
Ross, Stan, 50
Rothbart, Shire, 52, 113–14, 115
Rouhandeh, Jim, 149–50
Rounick, Judith, see Taubman, Judith Rounick
Rouse, James, 30–31, 38, 40–41
Royal Academy of Art, 141, 143
Ruprecht, Bill, 148
Russia, 126
Russian Tea Room, 44

Saks Fifth Avenue, 21, 43, 71, 73, 75, 78, 82, 120
salespersons, 65, 81, 116, 189
Salt Lake City, Utah, 198
Sam's Club, 83
San Francisco, Calif., 16, 22, 46
San Jose, Calif., 20, 23
Santa Barbara, Calif., 20
Sara B. Getty Foundation, 122
sausages, Hungarian, 61
Scanlon, John, 150
Scardino, Albert, 126–27
Schaumburg, Ill., 23
Schout, Bob, 49
Sconing, Warren, 46
Sears, 16, 18, 19, 21, 23, 46, 73
Sears Towers, 46
September 11, 2001, terrorist attacks, 161
serial vision, 34–35, 102
712 Fifth Avenue, 79, 121
sewer lines, 13
sewing, double-stitch vs. single-stitch, 4, 80
shoe salesman, 4, 6–7, 89
shopping center companies, 20–21

shopping centers and malls, 13, 15–24, 74, 109, 119, 127
  anchor department stores in, 13, 16, 19, 23, 33–34, 36, 43, 59, 66, 67, 71–72, 73, 120–21, 193–94
  as department stores of stores, 24, 44
  discount, 80–83
  effective advertising of, 33
  enclosed, 16, 21, 24, 39
  extended business hours of, 59
  financial architecture of, 42–44
  food courts in, 59–60
  food offerings in, 22, 59–61, 63, 72
  ice skating rinks removed from, 70
  Internet sales vs., 188–90
  luxury retailers in, 73, 75, 80, 88
  as new commercial downtowns, 23
  parking at, 13, 36–37
  promotion of, 44
  sales-per-square-foot of, 120–21
  size of, 16, 21–23, 120
  size of stores in, 16, 19, 21–23
  specialty stores in, 22, 43, 66, 72, 142
  strip, 12, 20
  suburban, 16–24
  tenant leases of, 38–39, 42–45, 142
  urban, 119–21, 193–94
  vacancy rate at opening of, 44
shopping centers and malls, design of, 24, 27, 30–41, 97–98, 106, 121
  anchor department stores in, 33–34, 36
  art in, 38
  as barrier free, 37
  ceilings in, 37
  court areas in, 38
  enclosure in, 39
  evolution of, 25–29
  flooring in, 37
  impulse buying and, 39, 44
  interior lighting levels in, 37
  lease renewals and, 38–39
  merchandising control in, 38–39
  multiplex movie theaters in, 39
  pedestrian traffic in, 36
  retail "undulation" in, 36
  ring roads in, 37
  sensory impressions in, 37–38
  serial vision in, 34–35
  skylights in, 37
  upper and lower parking in, 36–37
  upper level in, 36
shopping patterns, 18–19, 21–22, 120

Shorenstein, Walter, 7
Short Hills, N.J., 120–21
silverware, 81–82
Simmons, Chet, 112
Simon, David, 180–82, 187
Simon, Herb, 20, 21, 180
Simon, Melvin, 20, 21, 180
Simon Property Group, 179–82
Sims, 4, 10, 28, 109
Singer, Isaac Merrit, 28
Smith, Adam, 166–67
Smith, Earl E. T., 92
Smith, Joan Irvine, 48–49, 51
SmithGroup, 197
Smithsonian Institution, 84
Solomon Equities, 79, 121
Sotheby, John, 86, 136
Sotheby's, ix, x, 84–94, 95–108, 109, 134–45, 121, 127
  Arcade venue of, 105–6
  art market share of, 87–88
  assets of, 88, 93
  auction catalogues of, 98, 100, 106
  auction categories discontinued by, 101
  auction process of, 89–90
  branch offices of, 100
  as British national treasure, 92–93
  business areas of, 102–3
  Café added to, 98–99
  celebrity sales of, 106–7
  Christie's relationship with, 141, 142, 143–45
  collecting popularized by, 107
  in contentious takeover battle, 87, 90, 92
  credit offered by, 104–5
  disclosure of guarantees at, 144
  display techniques of, 106, 116–17
  employees of, 89, 93–94, 101, 149, 151, 170
  establishment of, 86, 98, 134
  financing policies of, 102–5
  industry benefited by, 97, 107–8
  international advisory board of, 100
  international art registry created by, 101
  inventory risks lacked by, 89
  in London, 90–93, 98–99, 134–37, 141–45
  management buyout proposal and, 137–38
  marketing of, 100
  Modigliani's *The Dreamer* sold by, 116
  Parke-Bernet acquired by, 97, 98
  Preview magazine of, 100
  private individuals as customers of, 89–90, 101, 102, 103–4, 106

professional art dealers and, 88, 101–5, 106,
    107
public stock offering of, 101, 133, 138, 148
renovated space of, 98–100
restructuring of, 93
revenues of, 97
rudeness encountered at, 89, 93
senior managers of, 96–97, 137–39, 148
stock option program of, 101
Taubman's investment in, 92–93
threshold resistance and, 89–90, 93–94,
    95–96, 106, 108
traveling exhibitions of, 100
250th anniversary celebration of, 134–37,
    140, 145
van Gogh's *Irises* sold by, 104–5
Sotheby's: Bidding for Class (Lacey), 98
Sotheby's-Christie's price-fixing scandal,
    137–45, 146–60, 164, 185–86
antitrust laws and, 141–42, 143, 150, 167–68
bankruptcy threatened by, 149, 151
Christie's granted amnesty in, 153–56, 160
civil lawsuits provoked by, 149, 150, 151
civil settlements in, 151–52
commission schedules and, 142–43, 145,
    146–48
conscious parallelism and, 142
Court TV special on, 185
defense team assembled for, 149–50,
    158–59, 171
Mason's book on, 151–52, 154, 157–58, 169,
    186
press coverage of, 146
Taubman's polygraph examination passed
    in, 159–60
Taubman's resignation forced by, 148
Taubman-Tennant meetings in, 141–45,
    152, 156–58, 165, 166, 170
unjustified price-fixing charge in, 142–43,
    145, 152, 156–57
see also Brooks, Diana "Dede"; Davidge,
    Christopher; Taubman, A. Alfred, trial
    of
Southfield, Mich., 19
Southland shopping mall, 16, 19, 21, 59
Southridge shopping center, 36
specialty stores, vii–ix, 22, 43, 66, 72, 142
Speedway gas stations 14
Spivak, Judge Peter, 112
S. S. Kresge, 13
Stamford Town Center, 120
Starbucks, 112

Stella, Frank, 84
Stewart, James B., 153
Stewart, Martha, 76–77
stock analysts, 77, 78
store design, vii–ix, 8, 10, 14, 24
    "deep throat" entry spaces of, vii–viii, 39
    of The Limited, 45
suburban development, 16–24, 128
    ancient, 17
    highway construction in, 19, 21–22, 23–24
    land costs of, 119
    population growth in, 17, 23, 119
Sunvalley shopping mall, 16, 19, 42
    trade area of, 21–22
Swid, Stephen, 87, 90, 92

Tanenbaum, Myles, 114
Target, 74, 76
Taubman, A. Alfred:
    appearance of, 3, 90, 171
    architecture training of, 5–6, 8, 10
    art collection of, 6, 84, 101, 103
    background of, 1–2
    in *Business Week,* 33, 40
    China visited by, 124
    college years of, 4, 5–8, 10
    Detroit residence of, 67
    divorce of, 85, 86
    as education reformer, 62, 128–31
    ethical partners of, 139–40
    first name not used by, 5
    grandchildren of, 178, 200
    investment philosophy of, 126–27
    lawsuit of, 162–63
    on museum boards of directors, 84
    Palm Beach residence of, 66, 86, 162–63
    as parent, 85–86
    personality of, 10, 91
    philanthropy of, 127–32, 197–98
    in prison, 137, 147, 152, 169, 171, 174–86
    as professional football team owner, 109,
        112–16
    professional relationships of, 44–46, 50, 51
    public speaking of, 130–31, 134–37, 139–40;
        see also Harvard Business School,
        Taubman's lecture at
    remarriage of, 86
    responsibility for employees felt by, 12–13
    as salesman, 4, 6–8
    school years of, 3–4
    as store designer, vii–ix, 8, 10, 14
    Tibet visited by, 123–24

Taubman, A. Alfred (*continued*)
  as white knight, 67, 71, 87
  World War II service of, 4–5, 163, 175, 177
Taubman, A. Alfred, trial of, 161–73
  antitrust law and, 167–68
  appeal of, 164, 167, 169, 170, 171
  Brooks's false testimony at, 145, 147, 148,
    164–66
  closing arguments in, 165–66
  criminal charge in, 150, 160
  Davidge's false testimony in, 157–58,
    164–65
  exculpatory testimony excluded in, 164
  guilty verdict in, 168
  hearsay evidence in, 157, 166
  judge's attitude in, 163–64, 166, 167–68,
    170–71
  jury deliberations in, 168–69
  jury's threshold resistance in, 165–66
  Keith's testimony at, 156
  press coverage of, 161–62, 168–69
  probation officer's recommendation in,
    170, 171
  proposed HBO movie on, 162
  Rosa Parks and, 172
  sentencing hearing of, 169, 170–71
  Tennant prevented from testifying at,
    156–58, 160
  Tennant's "memo" as evidence in, 157–58
Taubman, Fannie, 1
Taubman, Gayle, *see* Kalisman, Gayle
    Taubman
Taubman, Goldye, 2, 3
Taubman, Judith Rounick, 85–86, 91, 146, 162,
    170–71, 178, 185
Taubman, Lester, 2
Taubman, Philip, 1–3, 9
  business enterprises of, 2–3
  reputation valued by, 149, 169
  as Taubman Company partner, 11–12, 14,
    121, 170, 198
Taubman, Reva Kolodney, 8, 13, 85, 86
Taubman, Robert, 13, 53, 85–86
  children of, 200
  father's imprisonment and, 175, 177,
    181–82, 185
  hostile takeover attempt and, 180, 181–82
  with Taubman Company, 121, 123, 124,
    162, 170, 181–82, 198
Taubman, Sam, 2
Taubman, William, 13, 53, 85–86
  children of, 200

  with Taubman Company, 121, 123, 124, 162
  in Tibet, 123–24
Taubman-Allen-Irvine, 51–55
Taubman Center for State and Local
    Government, 131
Taubman Centers, Inc., 20, 119, 133, 188, 196
  hostile takeover attempt against, 179–82
  market research of, 22, 62
  portfolio of, 182
  store planning and design department of,
    45
Taubman Company, ix–ix, 10–14, 52, 85,
    97–98, 114, 126, 162, 170, 198
  company parties of, 12–13
  expansion of, 15–16
  as family business, 11–12, 121–24, 179–80
  growth of, 198
  innovations of, 13, 14, 16, 24, 42, 43–44,
    59–60
  leasing brochures of, 27
  managers of, 139
  mixed-use projects of, 79
  planning by, 39–41
  public relations office of, 117
  short leases preferred by, 38
  start up loan of, 12, 14, 51, 198
  as UPREIT, 133
Taubman Investment Company, 139
Tavern on the Green, 44
Taylor, Elizabeth, 106
Taylortown Shopping Center, 13
television, 112, 126, 185, 189–90
Tennant, Anthony, 154
  indictment of, 156–58, 160
  price-fixing denied by, 157–58
  Taubman's meetings with, 141–45, 152,
    156–58, 165, 166, 170
Tennyson, Christopher, 150, 174–75
threshold resistance, viii–ix, xi–xii, 3–4, 8, 22,
    24, 28, 144, 198, 199
  analyzing, 95–96
  British, 60
  to company expansion, 15–16
  convenience vs., 6–7
  to downtown shopping districts, 30–31
  of fashion-conscious shoppers, 78
  hostility as reaction to, 126–27
  interpersonal, 91
  Iran and, 45
  of jury, 165–66
  lack of confidence in, 65
  to luxury retailers, 73

to real estate investing, 46
  Sotheby's and, 89–90, 93–94, 95–96, 106, 108
  vehicular traffic in, 32
Thyssen-Bornemisza de Kászon, Baron Hans Heinrich, 100
TIAA, 42
Tibet, 123–24
Tiffany (Taubman's stepdaughter), 107, 124, 200
Tiffany's, 73, 121
Tipping Point, The (Gladwell), 25
T.J. Maxx, 82
Townscape (Cullen), 34–35
trade areas, 21–22, 33
Traub, Marvin, 72, 74–75, 77
Trizec, 20
Trump, Donald, 44, 79–80, 115
Trump, Fred, 79
Tsutsumi, Seiji, 100
Tufo, Peter, 124
turnkey jobs, 12
Twelve Oaks shopping center, 45

umbrella partnership real estate investment trust (UPREIT), 133
undulation, retail, 36
United Brands, 51, 57–58, 63
United States Football League (USFL), 109, 112–16
United States of America v. A. Alfred Taubman, 161–73
  see also Taubman, A. Alfred, trial of
urban development, 29, 119–21, 193–94
  downtown, 16–19, 21, 29, 30–33, 37, 106, 119, 121, 128, 192
  population density in, 17

van Gogh, Vincent, 104–5
Vienna, Austria, 194–95
Volpe, Justin, 184

Wall Street Journal, 116, 182, 191
Wal-Mart, 74, 75, 77, 78, 80
Walsh, Tom, 181, 182
Wanamaker, John, 28, 65
Wanamaker's, 18, 69
Warhol, Andy, 107
Warnecke, John Carl, 121
Washington, D.C., 64–72, 97
Washington Post, 68, 70, 71
Water Tower Place shopping center, 21
Waxman, Seth, 171

Weaver, Sigourney, 162
"Wednesday lunch," 102
Weiser, Benjamin, 172–73
Wells Fargo, 50, 51, 53–54
Wendy's, 57
Westfield Properties, 182
Westmoreland, David, 85, 86, 90, 92, 137
Wexner, Lex, 45, 79, 92, 106, 140
Wharton School, 7
white knights, 67, 71, 87
White Panthers, 155–56
Whitney Museum of American Art, 84
Williams-Sonoma, 76
Wilson, Kemmons, 57
Wilson, Peter, 87
Wilson Foundry Company, 2
Windsor, Duchess of, 106, 107
Winograd, Bernard, 139
Wm. Rogers silverware, 81–82
women's specialty stores, vii–ix
Woodfield mall, 23–24, 26, 33, 44, 88
Woodland Mall, 23, 139
Woods, Tiger, 107–8, 112
Woodward & Lothrop (Woodies), 64–72, 87, 109, 139
  bankruptcy of, 71
  downtown flagship store of, 68–69, 70
  Kringle Bears promotion at, 70–71
  management team of, 66–69, 71, 72, 138
  proposed leveraged buyouts of, 66–68
  renovation of, 68–69
  retail competitors of, 68–69
  revenues of, 66
  strength of, 64–66, 68
  suburban branches of, 69, 70
  Taubman's purchase of, 67–69
World's Fare, 59–60
World War II, 4–5, 14, 17, 18, 19, 163, 175, 177, 194
Wright, Frank, 58
Wright, Frank Lloyd, 10
Wurstmackers (sausage makers), 61
Wyndham, Henry, 137

Yankelovich, Skelly, and White, 62, 96
York, James O., 16, 21–23
Young, Coleman, 128, 195

Zell, Sam, 7, 78, 80
Zuckerman, Mitchell, 105
Zuckerman, Mort, 125–26

NOTES

Page

17 Comparative density of U.S. vs. German cities in the 1890s, Kenneth T. Jackson, *Crabgrass Frontier*, Oxford University Press, 1985, p. 43.

17 "Our property seems to me . . .": Jackson, p.12.

25 "If Victor Gruen invented the mall, Alfred Taubman perfected it . . .": Malcolm Gladwell, "The Terrazzo Jungle," *The New Yorker*, March 15, 2004, p.120.

26 "Superb buildings, filled with . . .": Johann Friedrich Geist, *Arcades, The History of a Building Type*, The MIT Press, 1985, p. 10.

26 "One can divide the arcade into two broad categories . . .": Geist, p. 70.

34 "Let us suppose that we are walking . . .": Gordon Cullen, *The Concise Townscape*, The Architectural Press, 2004, p. 9.

35 "Suppose, however, that we take . . .": Cullen, p. 9.

40 "His expensive patent leather shoes . . .": Shopping Centers Grow into Shopping Cities, *Business Week*, September 4, 1971, p 34.

40 "Just look at this . . .": *Business Week*, p. 34.

74 "In the 1930s and 1940s, as I was growing up . . .": Marvin Traub, *Like No Other Store in the World—The Bloomingdale's Legend and the Revolution in American Marketing*, Crown, 1993.

98 "Graham Llewellyn knew that Alfred Taubman had taken control . . .": Robert Lacey, *Sotheby's: Bidding for Class*, Little Brown and Company, 1998, p. 236.

104 "Before long there was spirited bidding . . .": John Marion, *The Best of Everything*, Simon and Schuster, 1989.

122 "Forget the celebrity CEO . . .": Family, Inc., *Business Week*, November 10, 2003, p.100.

123 "With tight-knit family leaders . . .": *Business Week*, November 10, 2003, p. 103

127 "Indeed, like a rich uncle, Taubman has a history of helping families . . .": Albert Scardino, *The New York Times*, March 10, 1986.

152 "There wasn't any real evidence that they fixed prices . . .": Christopher Mason, *The Art of the Steal*, G.P.Putnam's Sons, 2004, p. 347.

153 "Prior to 1993, a price-fixer who wanted

amnesty . . .": James B. Stewart, Bidding War, *The New Yorker*, October 15, 2001.

154 "Chris [Davidge] is a chief manipulator with a capital C . . .": Mason, p. 355.

154 "I am writing to assure you . . .": Mason, p. 221.

157 "Tennant firmly denied that he told Davidge to fix prices . . .": Mason, p. 350.

157 "It never was a memo . . .": Mason, p.350.

157 "He [Tennant] had no recollection . . .": Mason, p. 351.

158 "Whether true or not, Tennant's articulate reflections . . .": Mason, p. 349.

166 "People in the same trade seldom meet together . . .": Adam Smith, *An Inquiry into the Nature and Causes of the Wealth of Nations*, Great Books of the Western World, Encyclopaedia Britannica, Inc., 1992, Vol. 36, p. 63.

166 "It is impossible indeed to prevent such meetings . . .": Smith, p. 36.

169 "We did coerce him . . .": Mason, p. 346.

170 "Then the glamorous Judy Taubman walked into the courtroom . . .": Dominic Dunne, Dominic Dunne's Diary, *Vanity Fair*, July, 2002.

172 "They are kept in federal courthouses across the United States . . .": Benjamin Weiser, Judge's Decisions Draw Notice, for Being Late, *The New York Times*, December 6, 2004, p. A22.

173 "There was the woman in Queens . . .": Weiser, p. A22.

180 "I discovered they were mostly the same people . . .": Tom Walsh, "Takeover May be Over but the Odor Still Lingers," *The Detroit Free Press*, October 9, 2003.

181 "Martin Cohen . . . who had criticized Taubman centers . . .": Dean Starkman and Robin Sidel, Simon, Westfield Drop Taubman Bid, *The Wall Street Journal*, October 9, 2003

191 Henry Ford's $5 pay and *Wall Street Journal* criticism, Douglas Brinkley, *Wheels for the World: Henry Ford, His Company, and a Century of Progress*, Penguin Books, 2003, p.161.